THE RECIPROCAL EFFECT

By Nicholas Crayton

THE RECIPROCAL EFFECT

ISBN 13: 978-0-9047444-5-9

ISBN 10: 0984744452

Cover art by: Joshua Dunbar

Published by:
Midnight Express Books
POBox 69
Berryville AR 72616

PREFACE

The purpose for writing this book is to give you, the reader, a parent, a friend, or concerned neighbor, the chance to understand the thinking of a misguided generation.

I accept my responsibility for the chaos that I have caused and I hope that in my lifetime, I may be able to save some lives. All of the people that have lost their lives to the streets cannot be permitted to have died for nothing. Their deaths must preserve the lives of others. I, myself, have lost 15 friends to this cycle of violence. If I am to truly call these men my friends, then I cannot permit their deaths to be unimpactful.

Through me and others, their spirits will live on in a productive outlet to save others from that fate. Some will call it survivor's guilt but I look at it as my duty to responsibility. I have no more life to give catering to death. No more room for irresponsible decisions that harm others.

With the exception of a few, most books written by prisoners, ex-gang members, or murderers, are about that person's specific life events. This is not about me. It is not to glorify the street life but to clarify the ideas and pressures that the youth face. This is not coming from the perspective of a psychologist or law enforcement, but from a man who lived in corruption and understands what is so captivating about the street life.

I sacrificed my life for all of the wrong reasons. Maybe now I can live for the right one.

ACKNOWLEDGEMENTS

We must recognize those that have had an effect upon us because without their influence, we may not mold into the people that we need to become.

This is dedicated to those that held sway over me and kept me believing in the good of humanity. If your name is here, you may or may not realize the impact that you've had upon me but know that you did and I am truly appreciative because without you, I may not have accepted who I am or my duty to humanity. I Love you and thank you.

The Divine Creator that has given me the passion to live is first. My mother Neecy and my grandmother Delores, who taught me structure and discipline. My uncle Jesse and aunt Cheryl who've always encouraged me to believe in myself. My brother Reico who helped me find my passion in life. My friend Demetrius "Gumbo" P. who showed me strength in friendship. My aunt Portia who treated me as her own. My pops Eugene "Mac" who encouraged my kindness. My brother Samuel F. who aided my path. My sister Apryl who never abandoned me and believed in me, love you. My uncle Gentle who always protected me. Michael Baptist who taught me pride. Emmet X Wright who taught me how to be a soldier for righteousness. My brother RuachiYah who is my twin dreamer. My beautiful homegirls, Di. Ma. Col. (Giggles), Da. Sol. (the runner), S. Brad.(funny eyes), Wen. O'sul. (the feminist), and my pasty buddy Kem. My homeboys Jerri P., the fluffy one that flies high, and the D.J. of Seg. Also, especially to my partners who have always stood up to me, Dr. Dick W. Starks and Morio Zefanyah Billings.

INSPIRE OTHERS...

AND YOU YOURSELF

WILL BE INSPIRED.

INTRODUCTION

My young Asiatic males, parents, activists, journalist and all those who sincerely care about the genocide of our youth that is ongoing in the city of Chicago. As I sit here and watch CNN daily News and listen to journalists report on "Chicago's Deadly Streets" trying to find and answer to why there's so much violence amongst the young people in this city. I couldn't help but to offer my personal experience and thoughts to this epidemic that is plaguing our youth who are the future of a people.

I am a young so called "Black Male" who has been incarcerated since I was eighteen (18) and now I'm in my early thirties. I too was one of those wayward young males who ran the streets indulging in various forms of unsavory behavior. There's not a single problem or easy solution to the myriad of problems our youth face today. One primary factor can be accorded to the lack of parental guidance followed by spiritual awareness and a holistic education which can be a benefit to a prosperous future. Needless to say, the situation of our children all too common epidemic that only helps to feed this deadly cycle. In my view, the number one causation of this fatal cycle is the lack of fathers in the home, single parent units and or no parental guidance (what-so-ever) ultimately leaving these unfortunate children to be raised by city, county or state agencies as we are all aware that this type of situation will in the majority of cases result in failure.

With so many Asiatic (Black males) incarcerated and those who have abandoned their children (responsibility) at a pivotal stage in their lives, usually, before birth. As a result we are brought up to dislike and despise our male image by some of our mothers because she felt abandoned to raise us on her own. This could be a part of the reason for the disregard and contempt for Black male life by Black males.

I believe that these are a few of the main reasons we have so much violence amongst young Black males. Speaking from experience, I grew-up in a household of mostly women, a little sister, three aunties and a grandmother. My father was present in the house, though, the truth of the matter is—now that I'm older (mature) and have a better understanding of these type of situations I can now see that at the time when I and so many others like me was at that stage in life where we start to get curious about the forbidden things in the society. I also can now see that my father really didn't know how to be a "daddy" who should have sat me down to explain key factors about life to me —if in fact he knew them himself. So, other curious young males like myself learned all the wrong things from outside the home while getting involved with the wrong people who really didn't care if I lived to see another day. Little that I knew I had befriended people of whom had come from the same walk-of-life, or worse than I had experienced and held the very same pent-up anger over their situation.

In order for our young men to prove that they are not momma's boys, we must try to shake off the vestiges of our inadequate up-bringing and to gird-up ourselves to face and compete in a world that has come to believe we should be considered as nothing more than a statistic. Moreover, too many of us refused to listen to our mother's good guidance and sound advice because, we wanted to prove to her that we can take the place of our fathers in other words, be the "Man" in the house.

This cycle continues to spin round and around and like I stated at the beginning, these situations stem from a multiplicity of causes, including, but not limited to poor education on behalf of the parent(s), the failure of the school system to sufficiently provide an effective education for the child, and already crime ridden community that has been saturated with drugs and violence all of which spells poverty. Needless to say, Chicago politicians, with its long sitting mayor, Richard M. Daley, at the helm truly do not appear to believe or care whether city resources should be used for these type of people situations and communities as described herein. Based on a history of insensitivity coupled with abusive treatment on behalf of Chicago's finest there exist no harmonious/friendly relationship between the Black community and the Chicago Police Department. For example, say you have a neighbor who's dealing drugs—a mother decides to send her adolescent/teenage son to the corner store (for whatever reason), while the child is on errand for his Mom there is a high probability that he may be accosted by Chicago police and even be planted with a small amount of drugs. For your information, the instant illustration is an all too common occurrence in impoverished communities.

These words are coming from a young so called Black male who has lived in the inner city of Chicago my entire young adult life before I was wrongfully convicted of a crime that landed me in prison before my eighteenth (18) birthday. With all due respect to the Journalists who trust what they are told by police, public officials and community activists as to what they think the problems are with our youth you must be mindful that these people do not live in the "Trenches", as such does not hold first-hand knowledge or experience concerning what goes on in these areas to qualify what they say as fact. Needless to say, unless we have forgotten, this crisis is a collective one that the responsibility should be bore by, but not limited to, the family unit, the church, members of the community, community organizations, the city government, citizens of their city, county, state and country.

I sincerely care about our youth, irrespective of ethnic heritage we all are members of the human(e) family and as such our leaders have claimed that we are a civilized nation, then why do civilized people chose to turn a blind-eye and deaf-ear to the people of whom are less fortunate?

Still today I see too many young males come-in-and-out of prison with no direction or understanding of what has happened to them or what is happening in their extremely difficult and complicated lives. Education is far reaching for these males and their chances of succeeding in life is understandably grim. Though, little do they know education is the key to a prosperous life.

The current Commander and Chief of the United States, President, Barack H. Obama, is the epitome of what a good education can achieve. I view President Obama as a genuine leader who holds the best interest of all American citizens at heart. This President's level of achievement could be the result of caring educators during his years of schooling. If the people (teachers) who are educating our children are not dedicated-committed to their responsibility — including caring parents who will take the initiative to prepare their child for learning environment whereby they will not be disruptive in the classroom. Furthermore, all children are 'hard-wired' for discipline and when they do not receive adequate discipline they will automatically act-out in an attempt to gain the attention/discipline of the parent or guardian. After this overt, but yet, silent cry for attention is still not noticed or put into check the wayward child may only fall farther into the abyss of life.

This all comes down to the fact that there need to be programs implemented for these type of situations which will provide parents with the information knowledge of how to sufficiently raise their children. In addition, parents who have a child or children should not seek to be a "friend" to their children----children need proper parenting that encompasses Love, etcetera. If I'm able to see the problem so clearly, then, WHY can't the politicians and other so called leaders see it as well?

Simply put, we cannot change or fix the damage done in the past. More importantly, the ones of US who are in a position to effect change should at least possess a desire to do something about our tomorrows in an attempt to save the future of a people, the children.

I sincerely want to thank you for your time as well as concern in reading my lengthy commentary, and further wish to inform you in that, in the event that you desire to publish this writing or any portion of the same I respectfully ask that its contents should not be distorted. I also welcome your reply.

Thank you again.

Respectfully Yours,

TYREESE ROBERTS
Ill. River Corr. Ctr.
P.O. Box 1900
Canton, IL 61520

CHAPTER 1 The Plight

In order for us to understand the plight of the youth, we must know its origin. What does it mean to reciprocate and what makes it important to you? It is simply an interchanging between two objects, like an agreement; it sort of sounds like the "Golden rule", right? "Do unto others as you would have them do unto you". Well, it is a little more delicate than that.

This is written, not to be burdensome, but to help you understand if you can affect these kids. I have come to learn that being just a nice person does not move everyone. Being likeable is not the only factor in moving forward. Although, having a good character attracts people to you and allows them to be genuine with you, there are still certain qualities that you must possess so that you are not taken advantage of. People can see the light that surrounds you, even though you may not be aware of it.

The rule of reciprocation is seen all around us. We exhale carbon dioxide, which plants inhale. In turn, they give us oxygen which we know is essential to live. There is a mutual relationship between us. Let us take your job for example. You are paid an amount according to the service that you perform. You, the employee, provide your skill and the recipient pays you with currency that you use to provide a home or food. The relationship between two entities is in everything. There is no such thing as absolute independence. We are all bound by something. Whether we are acquiescing to God or man, no one is completely autonomous. We are all dependent on something or should I say interdependent. In one form or another, we depend upon one another for some type of need or aid. We depend upon our farmers to produce food for us. We depend upon big companies to produce good products for us and in return, we give them our business. We depend upon our governments to make the right decisions for our livelihood and we continue to elect them with our trust.

There are rules in which everything must obey or there will be consequences. If the earth did not regenerate its resources, we would die. If our immune system did not attack harmful micro-organisms, we would die. We must recognize and appreciate those things that we are dependent upon, especially other people. We must stop giving in to reckless desire, to spontaneous thoughts without conscious circumspection of our decisions. Where do you suspect that our children are getting these ideas from? We are designed as intelligent beings. It is time to start promoting this ideal in every facet of our lives.

Humans are naturally emotional beings and sometimes we don't know how to express ourselves properly. Look at how men are forced to suppress any sign of emotion because it is seen as a weakness (although anger is frequently expressed). We must use positive expression with our emotions if we are to curve violence. Men must come to realize that there is no weakness in understanding your emotions. Men are not emotionless beings. Human evolution, spiritual inspiration, and family bonds all require emotion.

Another thing that people say is that your environment affects you. I agree, but how does it? It affects who you are and what you will do. Indirectly, you will either separate yourself from it or you will directly take control and move forward. If you are raised in an unfriendly environment, you will either succumb to that erroneous way of thinking or you will become so fed up that you will do whatever is necessary to free yourself of that place. Unfortunately, many do not realize that they are capable enough to succeed in the latter.

So, how can we get the youth to realize how great that they really can be? How do you take hold of someone that has no hope, no pride, nor any faith and prove to them the greatness with which they can achieve? They need someone that is just like them to believe in. You must make them a believer in life because you are an example. Your passion must shine so that they can feel it as well. The effect that you have upon them must be so direct that they will desire to be better because you believe in their ability to be so.

Reassure them and they will learn to believe in their abilities. You are critical to their inspiration.

Some people believe that education frees us. I agree to an extent. Being just educated has its own bounds. Being educated in what and knowing how to use it are key factors in determining a person's freedom. We have to spark that gift that has been given to us since our inception. Our world is decaying and as we appear to move forward with technology, we appear to move backwards humanistically.

Many of these teens are choking themselves and cannot see the relative effects that they are causing to their minds and bodies. If it is not something that affects them at the moment, then they have no concern for it and when something does pop up, once healed, they quickly forget.

Society is so locked into the idea of death that most of the youth perceive this as a pass to live fast, die young, and go to eternal bliss life. This ideology is poisoning their minds. They have this idea that they need to fulfill every desire and pleasure with no consequential actions. They do not believe that they will suffer nor be punished for their youthful recklessness. They are actually desensitized to the world that they belong to. To them, life is only a haphazard mishap of some live, some die. Thus they mimic the ideals and values placed on T.V. (which would not be so bad if they

4

were not caught up in the fantasy of it), which eventually leads them to suffer from its extremities.

Some people are said to be inspired by God. Others may be inspired by reasons, or persons, or greed. People need to reach a certain level of inspiration to succeed in life, and teens are no different. There are numerous ideas being sold, broadcast, and fed freely on how people can change their lives and do better but the reality is that if a person does not study themselves and use their potential, then they will never be satisfied with who they are. A person has to choose to live a better life if they are to succeed in growing into the person that they desire to be.

Humanity has incurred much that has become harmful to itself. Instead of procuring that which eventually leads to heartache and destruction, we should be accruing life. Our right to live is innate in our DNA. We are at a precipice in life. The strength of a person lies within the consciousness of who they are and their duty in life. Money loses value, property and land can be taken away, yet a person's intellect can save them. This true treasure that will either save life or destroy it must be appreciated in its true form; through sincere action.

We are comprised from the elements of the earth and insured with the breath of God. Our inheritance is life. A person's ability to understand is the greatest gift that they have received from creation.

Our ability to learn and reason is amazing. The capacity that we hold to receive information is a gift itself.

Position, pleasure, and wealth are all things that can be taken away but the intellect from God cannot be commandeered unless allowed by you. We must show our children that when things appear to be angled towards your inevitable failure and destruction, you must become conscious, strategic, systematic, and scientific. Just as the earth contains rules in which it must obey so does humanity in all of its uniqueness. A person must prepare for all eventualities, whether they are spiritual or physical. I know that this may sound a little premature, but we are in a de-facto state of emergency with our youth, ourselves, and our Creator.

We must teach our kids how to free themselves from those things that direct them in failure. In some instances (like drugs and crime), we must show them how to hate that which is harboring them to live. They must make it their enemy instead of their comforter. Stop giving it justification and you will stop giving it power. Compare where they are in their lives and where they would like to be. Are they happy? If they do not care about their lives then they are definitely ill. They must be freed of those things that restrain them. Take time to learn about those things that stress them, impede them, and frustrate them. Certain obstacles do require more work than others but the goal is still the same. To better them from the point in which they are currently at.

Our youth are watching us intently. The plight that we find within them is with us. We have forsaken our principles and those instructions that help us. We tend to forget about the simple, important things as we are moving in such a fast world. Everyday our world evolves, as we do (or we should), but we must not allow ourselves to forget that this is our world and we must appreciate it so that it can appreciate us.

The plight of the youth does not lie so much in our money, home, or relationships. The economy in its horrific state is only a reflection of us. Our inner being as a people, a nation, a world is out of balance. We have allowed ourselves to become too relaxed in our discipline. We are no longer compelled to resist the things that we do not need. We have lost control of who we are and our children have naturally followed.

Do you really understand the importance of laws, rules, and instructions? You may think that they simply give order; maybe just to keep the disorderly in line. Maybe they just give structure to a society. Well, they certainly give balance to any system but more so they give focus and direction to a system—a system that is built upon the ideas of people who share solidarity in life. The law is not for convenience. It is to save your life. The youth see the law as an oppressor because they don't understand its value. We always talk about freedom as if there is no need for law in a civil society; this is misinformation to our children. They must understand that the law protects those that live within it and does not burden those that follow it.

We have lost faith in our government, our companies, and each other. It is difficult to trust people today. It appears as though that everyone is disloyal. This is part of the reason why violence has escalated in the streets. Everyone suspects everyone else. There is no brotherly love (if there ever was such a thing). This happened because the dream of our perfect country has become clouded in madness. We have become so masked in a dream that our reality has become decadent.

The media shows us the ugliness that is plaguing our homes. There are hours of tragedies, misfortunes, and scandals for our entertainment. We are fed ongoing investigations of horrible crimes and villains we have never known to exist. The media though, only shows us what we desire to see. We consume the gossip, the crimes, and the catastrophes. We have become predators of negative information. We are in a way addicted to bad news. For some people, it seems to make life a little more interesting. Crazy, huh? Well, ask yourself what do you mostly watch on television? How many hours do you dedicate to the gossip?

Another crack in our system is the onslaught of corruption that creeps in and out of our governments. We see it every day on our televisions and are disgusted by its implications. Our governors are speaking with the verbiage of a 1940's gangster. Our senators are passing tax laws yet neglecting to pay their own. Every day we see more reports of people failing to do their jobs or civil duties and we wonder has morality fallen. We are awestruck at the boldness of some people to actually commit such atrocious acts. What do we do? Give up on people? Of course not! We as humans must recognize that the propensity to do right or wrong is within us all but the choices that we pursue and actions that we perform will attest to who we are and define us. We must begin enforcing humanistic laws if we desire for our children to do what is right.

Do you know your state representative or senator? Did you vote for them? Begin learning about the people with whom you have placed your trust and make sure that they know who you are. Make them become transparent so that they have no room to commit fraudulent acts. We have failed in our duty to keep order. The people must maintain the spirit to keep the morality of the dream a reality.

We are a working unit. Do not become inept in your service to your community or your country. We all desire a better world. We have to work for it. Remember, we make the leaders who they are. Their strength lies in our ability to believe in them. You are the source of their power. Their persuasiveness is only as effective as you allow it to be. Do not give away your power so freely. Make them earn it because you and your family deserve it.

Do not be so quick to dismiss things that do not affect you directly. Do you really believe that the guy across town, robbing and selling drugs, does not affect you? Well, your tax dollars are affected by it. Every state in this nation is in a budget crisis and the penal system requires an adequate amount to function. This hits your wallet or purse directly. You may say "Well, that is okay as long as they stay on their side of town". The problem with that idea is, "What about your children?" Are they safe from the wave of criminals that are battling over false ideologies? They see the videos, the records, and the movies. They are influenced by their peers whether you see it or not. Who do you think that they really set their standards by when you are not around? There does not need to be trouble in the home for them to be led away from your grasp.

In this country and in the world, what we do can cause a rippling effect and if you have never believed it before, surely the recent world recession should have been more than enough proof. We must stop being incapable or inept to do our jobs as parents, friends, brothers, sisters, and very importantly, neighbors.

Our plight is the same. No matter where you are in the world, the struggle is still the same. Suffering and pain, happiness and peace, cross all barriers that we place in the way whether they be of hue, religion, or arrogance. The point remains the same, what you do effects me no matter where you may live. We must work together if street lifestyle problems are to be overthrown. Some plights require the shoulders of more than one person or nation. Some burdens must be shared by friends and neighbors so that victory can be achieved.

NICHOLAS CRAYTON

CHAPTER 2 What Is Happening?

Now this appears to be the question. What is going on? Let us take a look at the youth today. Their world seems to be so distant from ours; their ideas, language, and technology. Why is this? We were all young at one point but not all of us continued on in our youthful errors. Why do our new generations appear to be getting worse?

We as adults have made a great mistake. We have attempted to make the perfect, carefree society in which our children did not have to face the calamities that we and our parents did, and in doing so, we have indoctrinated a fabric within our families that does not require children to respect that which is right.

In essence, they have been spoiled out of common sense. Even in the lower income households, all they see are the riches that they equate with success and happiness. We have created a gap between appreciation and happiness.

In this social-networking age, children, teenagers, and young adults are living in a fast pace where everything is made available to them. Many have not had to endure the oppressive conditions that their parents had to in order to produce the life that they have become accustomed to.

In all of our cultures, our youth are not as appreciative to their history, land, or native tongue. We have to revive the spirit of pride to see the greatness in the future. If adults cannot aspire to be better, then how can we expect our children to be better leaders for tomorrow?

Where there is boredom, bad thoughts are born. Where there is no communication, violence arises. Two very serious issues that these kids have no experience with are boredom and communication.

Boredom is a dangerous thing, especially to a person that has no direction. Their minds can innovate some of the most deceitful ideas that may not appear so dangerous at the time, but once applied, they could be disastrous. A lot of us seek excitement or a sense of fulfillment in our lives which can lead us vastly astray. Our children are no different. They are anxious and active. So ready to grow up and sometimes gangs seem to give them a place in the world. I say "place" because their position is justified by where they stand. They see the glamour of T.V. and attempt to duplicate it. We always say that T.V. molds our society but we rarely talk about how it is really being done.

Let us look at the streets for example. Some of you that are reading this have never experienced the street life, but I can tell you this, that the things that are propagated on T.V. are not always true.

A lot of the time television influences the streets. Yes, it is true that a lot of violent things have happened in the streets but there are quite a few urban legends out there. These people that are behind the scenes promoting the "hood" do not even understand the effect of the things that are being spoken. All of the black youth are not poor or searching for a family when they join a gang, just as not all white children are either rich "nerds" or "Trailer trash", as that stereotype goes. My mother is a nurse as was my grandmother. I grew up in a fairly nice neighborhood. I lived in Hyde Park and attended Kenwood Academy (where I was introduced to the gang). I chose to join the gang for the fame. It was more than just the money or the materials. It was the glare that they received from the admirers. I wanted to be more than I perceived myself to be. I am not saying that I could not have been deterred from the gang life, but I was interested in it. At the time, it was the only thing that held my attention. That is the real illusion. We thought that it gave us a sense of independence.

In our culture, we praise the villains. We like the swagger of the bad guys. We imitate their coolness. We are in awe of their secrecy and humbled before their power. I believed that the lessons that I was being taught were valid. The struggle initially was for me and my family's benefit (or so I was told). If you are manipulated into believing that what you are doing is how things go, then you have no problem doing what is necessary. We were trained to believe that the "opposition" on another block or another part of the city was a threat to our survival. This aided us in committing such atrocious acts. We were conditioned to protect our leader's interests, even though they were not our best interests. You are duped into a false sense of duty.

Now the era in which I was assimilated into the gang was probably the last generation to receive any form of structure. The bangers today have no direction and no direct purpose. At least we had some sense of principles that we would not cross. Even the elders cannot control them. They only think about being a rebel and being rich. That is the absolute of their theology. Their legend is to be infamous.

The reason why these gangbangers are so out of control in the inner city is the same reason why the teen in the suburban area could be so easily taken by these people. It is the influence of the times. That same influence that enticed them into the madness must be the same to bring them out. Let me clarify. Police officers, politicians, and church leaders are not perceived as role models to these children. They are seen as the enemy. They are not a deterrent because it is taken as a challenge when they are confronted by these people. People are naturally influenced by others that are near their age or have similar values. This is no exception for children. What other children taught me was important to me because I feared isolation. It is not always the home that is the problem. Sometimes outside influences are so formidable, that trying to resist it with an ill-equipped mind, is very difficult. You see it all the time in the news; people do not understand or know how to stop the violence. That is because they themselves do not know how to unattach the grip that holds onto these bangers. They are misguided, yes, but bringing them out of this madness is not a simple dosage.

You must understand that it will take robust and focused leaders to have an effective impact amidst the chaos. Those that taught death must now teach life. It must be more than an awakening, more than some revolution, but more so a new position solidified within the parameters of making the conditioned mind understand how to live. The passion of these leaders must be evident so as to shine on others. Only a force that can challenge the relentless attitude can hope to persevere. If no one challenges them with results, why would they change?

What has happened? We have become inept in the affairs of our communities. We are too relaxed when it comes to our children and freedom is confused with carelessness. I can do whatever I want and mommy and daddy will save me. It takes for us to retake control of our communities. We must make up for what our neighbors lack and work together for everyone's benefit. If your neighbors' child is in trouble, don't be afraid to act. What affects your neighbors' child today could destroy your child tomorrow. Trust me; peer influence is a powerful motivator in making decisions when you are young. You must be involved with the affairs of your children. The dangers that you do not see are the dangers that you have a right to fear.

It must be realized that this is not just a black problem.

Chaos is not restricted to low-income whites and Latinos. Just as these threats are crossing class and color barriers, so must our passion and concern. Good and evil are decisions. We must make the choice to do what is right. We must be effective enough not to allow bad things to happen because we are afraid to face them. It is our right of responsibility to reclaim those things that are important in this world, those things that need protection, those that need guidance, and those that cannot be forsaken. I enjoy referring to the story of Joshua when discussing abandonment. In chapter 1, Joshua is given command of the army of Israel. He is instructed to prepare for the crossing of the Jordan River. In verses 14 and 15, he is told that he cannot forsake his brothers. He must help them to obtain their inheritance. He could rest once his brothers received their rest. This is an instruction that I believe is relevant today. We figure that these things do not affect us directly, so who cares? But this constant neglect has only allowed more violence, greed, and Ponzi schemes to spread throughout our society. This economic recession is only one example of how we have become unaware in our lives.

Self-interest is the force that propels capitalism. I get that. We need that for the system to work but we have become so selfish in this that we forget about our humanity. In a gang, you are taught that your brothers are priority. You would die for one another. As history teaches us though, too much depravity in power will unravel anything. Now the gang's self-interest is driven more by greed and selfishness. Outsiders are not telling on these guys, they are killing and telling on each other. They are devouring each other for their own preservation. They believe in the same dream as any other American, difference is, they don't know any other way to achieve success. Being an entrepreneur is impossible to them, why? Because their circumstances teach them that they are of less value than other people. They see the wreckage of their neighborhoods and believe that they are unworthy of anything greater. They are fragmented in their thinking and may be unconscious of it. I know because I believed it at one time. Chicago is infamous for its gangsters and corruption. We idolized it as holy. This is what we are and we must keep the title up.

Communication is also a great problem within many settings. Many of us, as men, have a difficult time communicating to one another for fear of not knowing how to speak to each other or we may be worried that we may be seen as weak. Some of us perceive it as unmanly to talk about our problems or disappointments. We look at it as feminine if we express ourselves to one another. We have been tainted into believing that it is the lesser man that speaks of his feelings. Men express themselves just as much as women do in private. I know because many have sat down with me for hours discussing their fears, joys, and passions. The problem is that many men cannot tolerate their pride being hurt. A man can sometimes express himself to his friend but find it difficult to express his thoughts to his woman. Why? Because in his mind, this is not a safe position. Thus when he is vulnerable and exposed anger is the key to restoring his pride. With his shell breached, he needs to raise his security. This is what is passed on to our boys. Our reluctance to be humble, to listen, or to say, I'm sorry. So what do they do? Harbor their feelings and explode in violence to release the pressure that was confined. That is what is easiest for them. This is not seen as weak because anger is not seen as an emotion.

Reticence (non-communication) is a dangerous silent code a-mongst the male gender. When there is no verbal communication between people, the wrong ideas begin to come into existence. We perceive every move, every eye, and every breath, as that of aggres-sion. Take two men that live in a room that is 8' by 14'. There is one sink and toilet. There is bound to be quite a bit of noise in such a small setting. If there is no communication between them, and one of them is awakened by a simple noise, the other person will take it as an intentional act although the other may have attempted to be courteous. If they do not talk about the situation, then resentment sneaks in. With nothing to occupy a man's time, his mind can conjure up things that are not real. Bitterness will follow and this can engulf a man whole if he entertains these negative thoughts long enough. Say that these men must stay within this room for 18 hours a day. They are trapped with themselves.

They are forced to face everything that they have done and everything that they are. Without any positive encouragement, they are faced with the reality of their situation. They do not consider that time is passing away from their lives and that they are wasting it. They become angry and frustrated, and without a focused outlet, they usually look for someone more vulnerable to escape the feeling of being trapped. Sounds like a prison setting right? Yes, it does but it is also the description of a man who does not know his role in life. His cellmate is that other half of his conscience that he must face day-to-day. He will look at him with either fear and submit or courage, and withstand the treachery that he imposes.

These kids are in a battle. They only reflect what they receive and they are afraid to explain what is infecting them (if they even know). I was watching a program about Kenya's T.V. programs and they discussed the anger between the tribes. They do not specify particular tribes on these programs because it may spark violence. The American journalists almost seem to snicker at the thought of this as it couldn't possibly make someone violent. But I understand that she has never been exposed to this type of experience. I agree with the producer. When you have separation through tribes, it can be set ablaze very easily. A week later, one of the cast members was killed by a rival tribe.

I see the same thing with the gangs. Although with the gangs, there are no blood ties or ancestral pride involved. The same solidarity that unites them can dissipate that bond. Their creed is no longer to a sense of duty but to the idea of fame. The lines are already becoming blurred due to police efforts and disunity, but they are becoming more dispersed and unstable. Although there is no structure, this makes them more dangerous because of their fluidity. You can't destroy gangs without having another system in place to attract them. That is why you have so many hybrid groups springing up out of the larger groups. Now, there are no rules or barriers to keep them from devouring everything and everyone. One thing is for sure, all of the money within these groups is flowing to someone on top. There is always someone that has caused enough carnage to control the thinking of these kids; to inspire them on in this nonsense. And he has set up a committee, an assembly to protect his identity and he has continued to use this control for his own preservation. Every gang has one.

That is what is happening. It is not always just some cry for help or a terrible environment. The entire scope of a generation has been forged in the absence of genuine leadership and community unification. Sparse and sporadic sparks will only go so far. There must be an implosion within the culture to destroy the energy flow of these ideologies. This can happen through a system of community families working together to combat stereotypes and ensure their children's' survival with effective enforcement.

What Is It About Death? Chasing death

Our society as a whole seems to be obsessed with death. We see it in every aspect of our lives. Our movies, books, and even our religious beliefs gear us toward dying. Everyone is so prepared to die, so ready for eternity; so sure about the afterlife and their place in it.

Even if a teen is not raised in a violent environment that does not mean that they aren't seeing the tradition. To us, the greatest sacrifice means dying for something else. To die in battle is honorable. Dying for a cause or belief is heroic; but what about living? How much more is required to live?

How can we expect children to be tomorrow's leaders if they all die today or if we adults fail in our duty to teach them? Some of us pursue death without even realizing it. We tempt it and ridicule it. Our logic is that "everyone dies from something", so who cares. Yes, death is one of the absolute factors in the universe, but, why must you die from something that is provoked? Our children have been instilled with this attitude and so they believe in getting rich even if they die. They equate wealth with happiness and so wealth must be obtained at whatever penalty. All of the blame cannot be placed simply on cinema and music. Our culture was born in dissidence. We are shrouded in violence and excitement. As trends set in, we eventually do things to encourage it. It appears to give us meaning, feeling, and stimulates our minds. We become consumed by it until we are entirely desensitized to it. Our heroes are the gunslingers that solve problems through violence.

We have created an ideology that near death experience is exciting. It is envied by those that have the courage to live it. In our cinema and entertainment, the climax comes when the hero is almost slain but prevails at the end. He slays the villain and the world endures. This feeds our fantasies, our imaginations, and our sense of greatness. Not that this is the cause for violence but it allows us to understand that violence is okay for the safety of defending the right cause.

We promote public enemies and criminals as justified rebels, as heroes in the world, entertainment becomes truth and life becomes distorted. Style becomes a director of goals. I do not want to get too vivid with the violence but look at the way these guys shoot a gun. Drive-bys mimic the cowboys of the old west, riding horses while shooting across from them. They stand in the open shooting at each other as if they will not get shot like in a standoff. I'm not saying that because of cowboys that gangs are killers. I am just showing you that these kids only copycat what they see.

Even in our religious stories, evil is always overthrown by violence. So, is it good to invoke violence with good intent? Who can regulate this? It seems that we are really attracted to violence but why is it so alluring?

Young men are nurtured to believe that they must not be weak. It is okay to be the bully but not the prey. Young boys see the elements on T.V. and in the neighborhood as the identity of manhood. They are duped by the heroic romanticism of masculinity.

A myriad of professionals have stated that the problem is in the home. This is not always true. The fabric of our households is not necessarily broken, but the relationships (especially in low-income communities) are distant and disconnected.

Although racism is still a reality, many teens of the new generations have never experienced pure hatred because of their color. This impedes them from relating to the civil rights generation. Those young adults were fueled by survival of their immediate lives. This kept them unified for a purpose that was tangible; a common plight. The youth today have no direction in their path. Once the leaders were decapitated from the gangs, the authority that bound them was lost. The gang leader's desire for control (power) ultimately destroyed them and will continue to destroy future leadership. Any leader that holds their position through fear or violence will one day be challenged and overthrown. That is the cycle. All will fail because the foundation that forms them is faulty and will break. There is no strong solidarity in corruption. Once they are removed, it is like turning on the water in the faucet and then taking a hammer and knocking off the head. Now, instead of the water being concentrated, it spews out everywhere. The leadership, although ruthless and horrible, kept the soldiers in order the majority of their reign.

People must stop thinking that it is solely the gangs that are in control. Gangs come and go. These ideologies grow and dissipate but the idea of manhood evolves more and more violently as our culture does. This is pivotal to our understanding of what they are doing.

Acceptance, love, pride, family, respect, fear, are all anchored on the same pivot; they need glory/infamy to feel a purpose. To serve something greater than ourselves has always been innate within us as humans. When we are little, we want to be great. We desire to do things that we see as exciting. This same desire translates over into the streets. Hence, why do you think that so many of us want to be rappers, basketball players, etc? It makes us feel like somebody that matters in the world.

Chasing death is not limited to the physical extinguishment of life. Death is also relevant to the destruction of our spirits and relationships. When we kill our relationships with people, we begin isolating ourselves into more hatred. That is when the warning is at its height.

Why are the youth so angry? They live in a country of opportunity and Twitter. They literally have the chance to be anything and anyone that they desire to be. No matter the circumstances or deficiencies, there is room for all. Anger is a poison. There were times when I was so furious that my body was physically hot. I could feel the hatred, the emotion, and without a positive thought, violence manifested. That is because anger is contagious. You could be having a really good day and if someone enters your midst that is upset, they can infect you. The same is seen with crowds. The misdirection and emotion in a few can ignite fervor in an entire group. You've seen it in riots. It is not foreign. That same spark is in these gangs. I hate someone and so you must hate them as well. My rage was crippling me. When I looked at myself, I decided to figure out why I was so angry. I realized that I had to take out all of the other variables. Once subtracted, I was the remaining sum. I'd allowed everything outside of me to infect me inside. This allowed for my violent behavior to be acceptable in my thinking. Poverty only breeds gangs because suffering forms unity. They formulate for social differences, financial, safety, and now, boredom. Let me clarify a little. Everyone in the streets knows that when you are standing on a corner, in the middle of the block, or in a gangway, that you are a potential target. This is a direct example of chasing death because you know the danger. Everyone in this lifestyle knows that prisons are violent and that you could die, but they continue to do things that could get them locked away. Teens are more aware about AIDS and STDs, yet they still have rampant sex. They are encouraging death everyday and are invoking it with their speech. "Life is too short" they say, which is why they are trying to do everything right now.

Dying in the streets is not glorious but urban tales would have you believe that it is. They believe in the fame, the money, and the possessions. They believe that the gamble is really worth their life. The "game" is a chance worth attempting because individually, they think that they are smarter than everyone else and even though they could get caught or die, it is better to have a 5-year plan to make a million dollars than to have a 30-year plan working legitimately.

People keep asking why they're doing these bad things. They want everything now. They want the American dream of fortune. They think that they can really become wealthy with failed schemes. They have no idea what real wealth is. They only understand money when they can see it. They only understand tangible things which is why quick satisfaction is so high.

Our society promotes "live life by your rules" with colorful slogans. I'm not suggesting that you shouldn't live life happily, which is a freedom of God not just democracy, but there must be responsibility taught with this ideology. This is a free society but there is a point within our consciousness that tells us that something is not right.

I have viewed a lot of violence in the streets but one of the worst deaths I'd ever known is the one where a person knew that they were about to die and unable to avoid it. This man had a rare cancer. When he was diagnosed and became ill, I thought that it would be like T.V., believing that he would do treatment and live with it. I saw him after the operation and he was so frail. An oxygen respirator was bound to him and they had attempted to cut a tumor out of his chest. It had spread too much to save him. He explained to me that he would probably not last to complete his six weeks of chemotherapy. I froze and had no idea what to say. This man knew that he was about to die and all that he could do is wait. That was terrifying. And sometimes, that is what it feels like in the streets. As if you are just anticipating your death. We all spoke of how we could possibly die in that lifestyle and what we wanted done at our funerals. Through this man's calamity, he asked me to stay the course of life. That takes courage to face death and continue to provoke life. I admire such people that face these troubles and choose to fight for their right to live. Unlike those of us who shamefully throw away this gift for nonsense. Dying in the streets is not honorable or worthy of any sense of recommendation. Young adults need to know this and they need to know that we know this.

When the news reports that a specific gang is terrorizing a neighborhood, this spreads their credibility. When they see their faces in the media, this heightens their fame. Everyone knows them. They are now respected and feared. That is why prison is not a direct deterrent; it is viewed as part of the lifestyle; an accepted risk.

We, as adults, must strip away the honor of the street code. Right now, it is fragmented, unstable, and people are adding commentary to their fractured understanding of an already corrupted foundation. What does this equal? An out-of-control system. A lot of the new gangbangers that I encounter don't even know the origin of their gang or the reason for its inception. They are strictly about money or fame. Coupled with the influence of poverty or acceptance, they become more dangerous. I say acceptance because prisons are not just filled (at least in Illinois) with poor, unwanted people. The reality of prisons is not like those dramatized on T.V. If nothing else, it is boring and a waste of life. It is not a triumph, but an extreme failure. It shows that what you thought that you could get away with, you can't. I don't care if someone told on you or you told on yourself, the point remains that the sum of that problem means death. You lose. Your life is wasted and many times your mind becomes alienated from reality. Prison has saved a lot of lives though, not just for possible future victims, but for those that were involved in the extremities of that lifestyle.

As you grow, you begin to look at the things that you have done in your past and you become disgusted with your actions. You are disgusted with yourself for believing in the lies. Young and wild, you want to impress the world by living on the edge. You desire the admiration and the infamy. The elder generation that is still involved knows that this life will lead to a premature death. But they also know that as long as the youth are ignorant to their reality, then they can continue to turn a profit. When did the boundaries blur between loyalty and selfishness? When people found greed more fulfilling than love. These men understood at some point that they would not survive the onslaught of corruption, so they backed up, and kept others in their place. Teens are thriving on the fame of another while being their proxy. Flash some money at them and they are loyal to whatever you tell them.

As I do agree that mainstream entertainment must accept some responsibility for these events, the main point of responsibility falls upon those directly in the midst of these areas. We have stood back and allowed death to filter through in the disguise of freedom of expression. I believe in the Constitution of the United States, and I believe in the freedom of speech, but I do not believe in the freedom to spread fear and anarchy to its own populace. We are not protecting the youth by aiding them in their nonsense. It is not helpful to know what your child is involved with and continue allowing them to do it. This is not friendship. It is accessory after the fact.

The youth of the 60's and 70's had more claim to being angry and outraged. Racism was strong and the police were not afraid to show it. People of all hues were on opposite sides and no one wanted to surrender. Their structure at that time, whether black, hispanic, or white served a purpose; to protect your own. Today's gangs have no legitimacy because the world is more tolerable and willing to move forward in unison. These new gangs have no rules or agendas. They simply form together for erratic endeavors. They band together, fight together, and kill each other. It seems ridiculous in a time when there are stringent laws that protect people from any form of discrimination. So why do they justify their crimes through economic deficiencies? Because we continue to allow these kids to believe that to be somebody, you must be rich. Angry at their circumstances, it is easier for them to believe in a scheme then to work for 20 or 30 years.

Once they enter into this cycle, it is difficult to turn away from it, especially if they have lost friends to the cause. They feel bound in that instance to a duty to avenge their friend. Friends in the streets live together, steal together, and reveal more than they do to their own families. Once that is taken from them, they become hollow. They understand the severity of what they have entered.

Now they must become someone fiercer to protect themselves from fear and pain. The title that they build ensures their status but only until another challenges and takes it. No one stays on top. No one just retires without retribution. They are too busy consuming each other.

The excitement and money becomes addictive. This addiction becomes so paramount that all logic is ignored while reacting emotions make primary decisions. Your life expectancy is shortened by your constant spiral into the lifestyle.

When I see the gangs today, I see conditioned chaos. No morals, no concerns, and no conscience. They remind me of soldiers that are trained to go to war without a mission, a commander, or a war. I am not suggesting that they cannot be saved; it will just require more sacrifice then some are willing to invest.

You must realize that their assessment of death is illogical. You hear these rappers say that they are just telling their story. Granted, there are some bad things that people endure in these communities but how many times will the same story be told over and over? They are not simply telling a story, they are replaying a crime. This constant reiteration of death only symbolizes that their focus is on selfish achievements of making money. Everyone in these areas is not suffering. Everyone in the "hood" is not a gangster. The crap that is continuously being splattered across our screens as real, are just people making money while others wallow in pain. Going to jail does not make us any more cultured, cool, or clever. It is an embarrassment to us and our families. Thus, this is our duty to stop these kids from pursuing death.

What Is It About Death? Accepting Life

What is it about your life that makes you want to live? When we understand, we are able to appreciate. Kids believe that the challenge of life is so difficult. They do not realize the courage and confidence that they hold within themselves. When your children see your standards and the things that are beneficial to you, they pick up on it. They learn how to value things through you. Do not allow their values to be placed in objects but more into who they will become. This unseen force passes off to your children. They are watching and learning. Evaluate what is important to you. Determine what is beneficial and teach this to your children and their friends. As you accept the challenge of life, they will follow.

Accepting life does not mean accepting the way that things are. It means that you accept the challenge to live and to change those things that make your life miserable. Life must be worth living and the beauty of it must be shared. Express this in your home. Show them what the world really consist of. They need to know that poverty and pain are not restricted to their neighborhoods or culture. There are children that have never met other cultures or people of different hues. How can they be expected to accept others if there is no interaction? How can they believe that God created all equal if they have not experienced that equality through social relations? Are we really more civilized than our ancestors? Don't allow your children to become enslaved to ignorance. It can be just as deadly as the gun that is put into their hands. Show them how to interact with other people and build relationships. Remember, they mimic what they see, so if you are always upset and angry, they will be too.

As an adult, I sometimes catch myself doing or saying things that my mother does. I don't do it intentionally, but I am her, so it is in me to be like her. And that is not to say that I could not eliminate these attributes, but seeing that they are not bad traits, I appreciate them and her for being who she is.

The youth must understand that you are not forcing them to do what you want them to do. This only feeds their resistance. You are showing them what they are capable of doing. The ability to choose is appealing. Options will calm resistance. Be firm, not forceful. Support but do not accept antics with it. Whether you are a parent, a peer, or a neighbor, you probably hold some influence over this person's life and you should be conscientious in your support. It is not given freely. It is an investment given with a condition. That the person that it is being allotted to will choose differently, not dangerously. If you continue to feed them while they are doing negative things, then you are aiding their cause. Encourage their goals, not their recklessness. Accepting them does not mean accepting their depraved behavior. I understand that you don't want to turn your back on them, but if you allow them too much room for error, they will think that you are weak and unintelligent. They see the opening and will take it.

Why do you think that so many gangs have spread to so many unexpected areas? Parents believe that simply moving away from an infested area will help, but not necessarily; especially if your child is infected enough with the ideology to become a host. All they do is infect other areas. The fantasy of that lifestyle is brought to life by people who live in these areas and so others are enticed into it.

This is why I stress inspiring them out of the madness; leading them out of the chaos. The world is so busy and everyone with it. All of us seem to be so busy with our own problems that we neglect everyone else, even our children. I know parents that are good people, they work hard, but they are so unaware of the things going on in their child's life. It is difficult being a single parent and that is why I believe that help is required. Get more adults involved in your child's life if you are alone. You need the help. They need the help. This isn't a black problem or a poor person's tragedy, young adults all across this nation are falling into this madness even if they are not directly involved.

Earlier I wrote about boredom. When people are bored, they are unhappy. That is when misleading ideas have time to grow and power to persuade them. Help them find their passion so that they can understand what it means to have purpose. When these kids feel as though they have no purpose, they feel the need to fulfill another person's demands. They do not care about the consequences of the things that they are doing because they need to fill a void. Someone else will set the standard for them. The platform that someone else sets could force them into a bad position. That is how they spread. These kids think that they are finding friendship, acceptance, and loyalty. They think that they have found a legitimate bond with their crew. Now they have something to fill their time and their lives with. This encourages them to be loyal to a lie. You are their family. You are the person that they need to feed from. You are their happiness. You must also let them know that you need them. Some hate to see their mothers struggling and think that this is a way to help them. Some may feel as though their lives hold no value. Show them that their lives hold great value to you. Do not let them believe that their lives are of no value in this world. There are some that feel dead within themselves every day; dead in spirit, in hope, and those that have no one tangible to believe in. To them, life itself is a deterrent. Teach them to live for the living and not the dead (and not to die for the dead). Expand their view of life. There are many variables in life and different perspectives in which people view it. Guide them to see the happiness within the world. If at first they cannot see it, then make them feel it. Channel the things that they are happy with, the things that spark that energy and appeal. You can literally feel life. You can appreciate what it means to feel alive and so should they. We mustn't wait for some near fatal experience or loss of someone endearing to appreciate those things around us or in us. They must be taught the benefit of making good choices.

They need to accept their strengths and their flaws. You want to challenge what they believe? Then you must challenge the entire foundation of that system. You cannot do it by yourself. Work with your friends, community officials, and anyone else that has an investment in the community. Local businesses, no matter how big, need your support. So you make them give you theirs. If enough people collectively come together and tell these stores to support a neighborhood-protection program, they will pay attention. Use this to the neighborhoods advantage. An economic cycle should flow not just income, but innovation and support, back into the adjacent community. Stop thinking that you hold no power; the God that you serve has given you the strength and ability to live happily. Use the courage of the spirit to help you manifest truth.

These young people want to be someone worthy of renown. They need real examples of great people. They need to experience that greatness themselves if they are to be compelled to follow after it. Many people and things can influence our thoughts but if we are grounded in our desire to live and not just to survive, then we can find ourselves striving to be better at all times.

Look at how people migrate to this country. The appreciation that they have, the dedication that they hold and the patience that they show is impressive. They have survived the destructive forces angled at them and they want to live. To live freely and happily and they will work hard with sacrifice to maintain it. They are not spoiled by the American Dream, they respect it.

The same can happen when a person continues to live in a negative way and gets tired of failing, sick of jail, and has nothing to show for their life. They realize that they will never become rich from selling drugs, guns, or stealing. The reality of their life becomes depressing. Problem is that this usually doesn't happen until someone gets past 40 years of age. But, the proof is there. The failure-success ratio is so overwhelmingly mismatched that there is no contesting it. There is no happy ending in the streets but the movies and videos don't show this.

You know what I have come to realize? The time has always been at hand. It is time to stop accepting the way that things are going and know that we can change them. Waiting for someone else to do it will only prolong it and give death more room to feed. Putting your thoughts into action proves the power of God and of the mind.

Everyone needs a set of rules in which to live parallel with. All humans need guidance and help. The youth requires leaders that are not afraid of them but are not overly burdensome either. It is not about "being perfect" but it is simply about being a genuine person in their eyes that will make them respect you. They must believe in your ability to make real things happen. That when you tell them that they can do something great, it is not some fantasy, because you can show them how to achieve it.

How can you give your children a better life if you do not appreciate the one that you have? One of the most affluent slogans that you hear in these neighborhoods is "don't forget where you come from". Many people interpret this as when you get rich, you must still act "ghetto". And that is why we see celebrities performing in public as if they are on a block with their drunken friends. They actually believe that it gives them credibility. Not forgetting your past means helping those that you left behind. It is about strengthening the community that you struggled in. Our children see them and think "yeah, he is still hood". It makes no sense. You sell drugs so that you are no longer poor. You don't continue to do things that will cause you to go to prison. Jail is a chance that you take for achieving a goal. What kind of an idiot makes it successfully and then does something that will cause them to lose everything?

That is why persuasion must be fortified by positive engagement. There is no glory in saying "I'm poor", because if there was, so many would not be attempting to die for wealth. Growing up in harsh conditions does not make you as tough as so many believe. There are a lot of broken kids in these communities. There is a lot of depression. These street codes and concepts were designed to protect those that united to save themselves from that condition. It was not to keep them in the same condition that they fought so hard to leave.

Life is fun when you are not constantly watching out to protect it from your choices. They must be surrounded with life. Teach them their duty to life. Not some vague idea that they cannot comprehend. A real perspective made tangible through their lives. If you tell them that it is good to help others, then take them somewhere of perform this idea. Not simply with talking but with an application comes realization. If you tell them that life is not miserable, be an example. Get help from friends and neighbors. If you tell them that it could be worse, then show them just how bad it could be. Give them a reason to strive for better. Cultivate their passion so that it is clear for them. Do not allow their passion to be blanketed by fear of popularity. Their peers will not be there in the bad times, you will. You have the power to guide them appropriately.

I hear people say that these kids need love. While I do not dispute this, I do question the manner in which it is given. Love must be acknowledged but not to where it has no limits; loving them means enforcing rules. It means that you must direct their paths, even while they are unaware of it. You must not be compliant with their dangerous activities.

Accepting life means to accept the responsibility of someone else, even if they are not your family. You have accepted that every child is important and that their life can be saved. If people will come together and unify for that direct purpose of saving these kids, it can be done. They are lost in a pit of madness and they need help. It cannot be left unattended. It is not like some wound that will heal because of the natural design of the body. You are the immune system. You must activate the treatment if they are to be healed.

People must understand that although things do get bad, force will not quell the problem. It will not stop the drug dealers hunger for survival as he perceives it. This is how they live. This is their perspective of how to make a life for themselves. We must show them how to accept life, and move with life without being disruptive to it. There is no simple villain to this story.

Women And The Pain That We Cause: Demoralized

We, as men, really do not pay attention to the destruction that we do to women in our culture. We use them, belittle them, and toss them away as if they hold no value to us. Although throughout history, and in every culture and setting, misogyny has been involved, the street lifestyle is one of the most dangerous.

The identity of girls and women in this lifestyle is that of an illusion. The video girls or the bad girl image are the only positions set for them. They can be the one that entertains or the one that aids in a crime. The girls that are looking to be accepted are the easiest to deceive. It's interesting because some of these girls do not realize how much power that they hold. The boys want to impress the girls, no matter how much they may deny it. The attention from females is intoxicating. You want to do the things that will make them notice you. Many boys will chant the anthem that they do not care what girls think yet we act, dress, and think according to what will attract them. We do some of the most ridiculous things under the guise of impressing girls.

Our girls are beaten, raped, and forced to do crimes according to someone else's benefit. Don't get me wrong. I've met some girls that were tougher than some boys, but they only mimicked what they saw. Some of them began enjoying the terror that they caused. This was another indicator to me that evilness was not limited to one gender or color.

These girls have the desire to be beautiful. They want to be seen and desired by all of their peers. The idea of beauty has been perverted and turned into an unobtainable fantasy. Some of the boys recognized gender inequality at every age. You are taught that girls are not as important as you are. In many impoverished areas, girls are seen simply as trophies.

In many instances, we have misled women into depravity. We have made a path of deception in which they have attempted to fulfill, only to fail, over and over again. They have repeatedly changed their beauty, ideas, and lives to appease us yet we use this ploy to prove our dominion over them (or so we think). We have forced them to fulfill some fantasy that is not only distasteful, but unnatural. We cannot continue to destroy the natural beauty of women with our fists, our heartaches, and our disloyalty.

Some boys, and men, are misogynistic without even realizing it. Boys are trained in this manner when they are exposed to the demeaning language or attitudes that make women appear as less valuable. For teens in the streets, girls are viewed solely for their physical benefits. I do not just mean sex either. Drug liaisons, law-abiding tenets for drug houses or other frauds, and safe havens from law enforcement.

Violence, money, and women are all accredited as credentials. The more numbers that you tally up, the more that you are seen as a celebrity. There is no emotion involved with it because you become desensitized through your own sense of triumph and arrogance.

You are only concerned about the thoughts of your peers and the feelings of some girl are irrelevant. Why? Because she holds no real position in the streets. Teenage boys are following trends set forth by their predecessors, as when pimps were seen as strong, dominant men. Just look at the way that they talk and dress. They see these men as icons. Having multiple women at your call is an ultimate triumph of manhood. This has been a long time idea. This did not culminate with hip hop.

What I am clarifying is that men have (not all) belligerently destroyed the character of women throughout history. They were demoted to the position of slaves instead of their rightful position as partners. Some theologians have propagated that women are the tools for which the devil uses to afflict men. They are encased in a venomous scandal of sexual immorality and malicious intent. Can you believe it? Some of my "leaders" taught me that women were sneaky and untrustworthy. Funny thing is that most of the betrayal in my life has been from men.

Woman must stop being forced to suffer for all of humanities troubles. They are not the centers of evil nor the propagators of Satan's work in the world. Bad people are bad people by choice. Evil thoughts are evil thoughts and can be passed down to succeeding generations. The true identity of women has been stolen and must be returned or it will continue to infect our children and they will continue to destroy themselves.

What is it about a woman that a man feels so threatened that he must degrade her, abuse her, and even destroy her in order to maintain his manhood? Why is it that we, as men, are always suspicious as to their motives? Many times we manipulate them into believing our lies. We make them think that everything that we do is for their benefit and we tell them that we love them with the fluidity of oil, and then we disregard them at the sight of someone more tempting. We expect so much from our women and yet we take too much from them.

Many boys are taught that being a man is paying bills, supporting children monetarily, and saying that they love these women. We are misinformed that sexuality expresses appreciation. The problem that a lot of these men have with loving another person properly is that they do not understand it. The importance of expression is omitted when you are young. We are taught that expression is feminine and therefore weak. Men do not say what they are feeling because it is seen as soft.

When it comes to these girls that we get involved with, we neglect their interests, their feelings, and their thoughts. It is not as though we had any real experience with relationships anyway. As I said, we saw sex as the totality of a relationship. We ignored their words and drowned out their problems to keep us from feeling anything for them. We have allowed the feminine aspect of everything to be strained out of our lives. That side of the perspective has been taken from us and so we refute anything that is not of masculine content. Any sign of femininity is disavowed as weak or unintelligent.

Women must be more conscientious in not accepting the "titles' that they have inherited. Our daughters are watching and imitating what they see. These adverse slanders have made some believe that they are no better than trash. As these girls present themselves in this manner, the boys respond as such. Men will not treat them like a wife if they present themselves like someone out of a porno. Women must redefine this perception or men will continue to mislead them.

Boys often attempt to prove themselves to girls. Many of us performed for them. We were actors in a show, albeit it was real, we still did things that we would not have normally considered. We are like our animal brothers when it comes to impressing the feminine gender of our species. Although we may not collide horns or foreheads, our instinct for feminine approval can have us do some outlandish things.

Women must stop being scrutinized and set up for a standard that is morally corrupt. We expect for them to be submissive dolls at all times and when they cannot fulfill this ideal, we abandon them. These idiosyncrasies are deep within our culture and passed down to our children. Our girls must not believe that they are only here to look pretty and have babies. They also do not need to believe that their duty is to be better then every man.

One extreme to the other is unhealthy. Girls in impoverished areas that believe that they must compete with boys usually commit very bad crimes. They think that they must be more ruthless than the men. And sometimes they can be. They also try to protect these boys because they believe that they really care for them. The girls think that it is their duty to protect these guys. Their loyalty usually costs them more than they can afford.

There is abundance of great, female role models out there that are intelligent, humble, witty, gorgeous, and in control. When one woman does something ridiculous or outrageous, it seems to speak for the entire gender. We expect for men to do bad or stupid things, but if a woman does it, she is a representative of the nature of women as a whole; ridiculous at best, tragic at worst.

This process has been going on for centuries. It is not something new or astonishing, but what is sad, is that we pride ourselves on being a so-called developed society yet we continue on with some of our prehistoric attitudes.

Our girls in this lifestyle are just as pivotal as our boys in changing its direction. Do not believe that because your girls are not living in these areas that they are not influenced. Today, the bad boys craze is everywhere and these girls no matter where they live, are falling right into it. They want to be liked and they really have no idea of the dangers that come with that life. This is not limited to hue. Just because a black boy dates a white girl does not mean that he will corrupt her. But if a boy (no matter his hue) is deeply involved with the depravity and his girlfriend is unfamiliar with that lifestyle, she is an easy target. There are plenty of girls that have been raped, kidnapped, and murdered because of who their boyfriends were. There are girls that end up in prison because of their boyfriend's occupation. They are swept up in the chaos. There was a time when you were taught not to shoot if the target was unclear. No children were to be placed in danger. No mothers could be harmed. If you were with a female or your mother, you would get a pass. Nowadays, they kill girls and children no matter the consequences. Girls are no longer exempt from the violence even if they have no knowledge of it.

Girls that are abused in their homes are of course more susceptible to following the trend. They believe that they have no value and thus have no concern for their lives. In impoverished areas, there is also an absence of strong, feminine success. When all they see is their mothers, sisters, and other women treated better because of their lovers, they hold themselves to that standard. Others feel as though they must use men to achieve their goals at whatever expense. They have learned the "shark story" from their male counterparts. Why should they be without when they have something that all men want? To them, it is simply a tool to attract your objective. They think that it will be emotionless for them. They are often wrong about this.

Although girls tend to be academically smarter than boys, they lower themselves to please their boyfriends. This is very dangerous because they will do whatever to fulfill this duty. Some girls are used to hold drugs, others to acquire property for stash houses, and others simply for their monetary value. These girls are deceived by the publicity of the streets. There is no relative value for them in this lifestyle. They are used just as frequently as a cigarette.

Because we adults allow it to dictate our own platform, beauty is expressed through the feminine curvature or makeup. Femininity is debased to a woman's appearance. These girls feel pretty and worthy when these guys tell them that they are. Your daughters must not be allowed to fall into this trap.

Women And The Pain That We Cause: Appreciation

What is it about appreciating a woman that will bring balance back to our neighborhoods? Well, first they are the reason that a great many of these boys act out the way that they do. How do we show them our appreciation and to express to them that we recognize how critical that they are to our lives? Our girls are watching and we must show them that they do matter in this world.

In our evolved world, women are not perceived to be as oppressed as they have been throughout history yet the male dominated idea has not changed dramatically. You may study history as far as it will permit you, and you will understand that women have always produced a scintillating effect upon the world. They are our mothers, teachers, lovers, and most times, our maintainers of sanity.

Women are perceived to be emotionally weaker than men, when in some instances, they appear to be stronger. We perceive anger, rage, and frustration as not being emotional. Like men don't cry. So, it is okay for a man to express these attributes without being called emotional or sensitive, but if any other emotion is expressed, it is seen as "womanly". Boys do not want to seem weak, so they think that the attitude of aggression will equal masculinity. For years, women have been raped, beaten, oppressed, given birth to children, kept a job, and yet they continue to maintain their natural instinct for nurturing and caring. On the opposite side, if her male counterpart is harmed or disrespected, his instincts are to immediately annihilate something or someone for a sense of security or closure within himself.

A woman can suffer tremendously, yet she can continue to invoke kindness and be tolerable enough to endure harm without always allowing it to impede her as a person. Some men may try to assert that the women that they have known are not like that but I ask them, "Have you ever given them a reason to show you this side of them? Of whom they naturally are?" A really sad event is that these women are so precious as to tolerate the tragedies that we put them through and they continue to hold on to us. They cradle us when we do not deserve it, they sacrifice for us when they have nothing to give, and they love us when we have not earned it.

Girls hold the power to inspire or decay. Their power over boys is strong and sometimes difficult to resist. This is why boys are taught that women are evil. Women have been promulgated as being evil for centuries, continuously blamed for mistakes or misunderstandings as being blatantly malicious acts. History proves the lightening effect that women have had upon the world. Many of them have sacrificed just as greatly as men. The question that I pose is, "Why do we continue to destroy her?" As beneficial and life-giving as she is to us, why continue to harm her and in fact hurt ourselves? It is pure suicide.

I do not want to sound as if I am some relationship expert but I understand that the depreciation of the feminine gender in these areas is strong and entices boys to become more belligerent.

There is no effective communication between these boys and girls. Boys do not want to expose their vulnerability because of the manias passed down to them about the treachery of women and so he is taught to use them. This fence that they build only cripples them and keeps them enslaved to that idea.

The Divine attributes that interlock men and women are evident. From the physical, spiritual, or psychological points, we are perfectly fit to be bound together. There is no survival without the other and no peace in our separation. We can't look at one another with jealousy or prejudiceness. The act of appreciation must come with the idea of acceptance. If we do not accept that women have a defining duty to life, then we will not mature as we should as humans.

Girls that are lost in this terrible cycle will never come out of it unless they understand that they are not valued by their shape or how pretty their clothes are. Girls need that true feminine influence in their lives; that sincere essence that is being stripped away from them, not this cosmetic form of feminine virtue.

Real men must take a stand against crimes toward women. We must stand against these horrendous acts because just as the woman that you dislike can be raped and beaten, so can your mother, sister, or daughter (if they have not already suffered such a fate). This ill-cycle must be uprooted if we are to save our families. We must protect that which is important to us. Women must be reassured of their positions in this world. We cannot distort the duties of either gender as though we can make it alone. One cannot push forward through life without the other. We are designed to persevere together and this pride must be reiterated. This is not a competition between us although it appears that we have made it to be one. We must appreciate the roles of both genders so that we may continue to motivate each other. How can these kids do it if you are not doing it in the home? Why would boys want to treat a woman with any sense of respect when all they see is their father beating their mothers or the so-called pimps dominating these girls to make money? This is a social problem that is escalating into a virus.

The street lifestyle only plagues these girls because of the disdain that we show these women in our culture. And when I speak of culture, I am referring to American culture, not simply black or white. This incessant behavior of misogyny must be shamed and deterred. These girls must he shown the real value of their beauty. They must be released from the burden of the hateful scope placed on them. We must change the idea of womanhood in these areas. Successful women must invoke positive influences within the center of these girls view so that it is real for them. These girls require veritable support if they are to overcome the ridicule and pressure that they face. There needs to be weekly roundups of these girls to discuss their problems. They need help to leave these gangs, to know that they have support from more than just family members and that they have something tangible that will not forsake them when they are distressed.

One thing that is common in any part of the world is the bond between a mother and her son. A great many of these boys within these places see the struggle and the pains that their mothers endure, and this justifies for them, their wrongdoing. Although these kids can commit some horrible crimes, the reverance for their mothers remains. Even when you have those that are negligent or on drugs, the child still holds to the bond. Boys especially crave it from their mothers, no matter if they are teens or adults. That is a common linkage within the street life. People are always talking about these kids are in the streets searching for love but it is that love for their mothers, their families that sometimes pushes them out into the streets. If it is love that drives them, then violence from police and each other will not deter them. That love must be confronted with love. But it must not be some superficial, weak appearance of love. The mothers in these districts must be unified and assisted. They must be seen as the support in the lives of these areas. Although male leadership and models are critical, the mothers must be given back their strength. They must be seen as the defining barrier between the idiocy and reality. Even the toughest gangster reveres and cares for his mother. Ask any of them. They must be supported in order to guide their children intelligently. A boy never forgets what his mother taught him or the care that she displayed to him. But he also never forgets the negligence or care that she lacked. The respect for women must be returned to them through our actions.

This is the dichotomy of girls and boys in the streets; They only reflect the behavior that they have been shown how to treat one another. If adults respond to each other with more than spiteful remarks, our children will not be as malicious towards one another. They learn suspicion, misogyny, and disrespect from the most interesting places, and trust what I tell you, it is not always the T.V. that teaches them.

So, appreciate other people and show these kids that it does not make you weak or a joke to be nice to people. Make them understand that opinions belong to that person and no one else, even if it's in a book. Appreciate your kids and they will appreciate you back.

Why Are We Responsible? The Corruptors

Anyone that has committed a crime, anyone that has broken the rules of society, blatantly disregarding life, is responsible for the chaos that has been set. Those that have served in the streets were corrupted and in turn, corruptors. We to became leaders and mislead teens into dissident behavior. We are bound to correct these errors because in truth, why should society care about those that have afflicted civil order?

Many times people blame their environment for the crimes that they have committed and the judgments that they have made. This can be accepted as some of the reason but not in totality. This vulnerability to fit in with the crowd is a strong force in many of the decisions throughout our lives. We follow the newest trends and want to stay in accord with the rest of the world.

I personally had the chance to do some great things. I lived in Hyde Park, went to Kenwood Academy, and I always had numerous places to live. So, with all of the support, how could I fall off of the radar? Like I said, there are multiple factors but the most prevalent is indebted within our culture; Acceptance; the desire to feel wanted and needed. We all have this innate feeling. Everyone wants to be seen as somebody special. Whether through notoriety or popularity, we will do whatever it takes to fulfill this desire. You don't have to come from a broken home or dysfunctional family setting to desire to feel important. Isolation is difficult no matter your background. Our quest for fulfillment is born with us. It is most evident when we are searching for God and we want a personal relationship with our Creator. It is through our connections that we feel happy and whole. Deprived children and teens are especially capitulating to this feeling.

The gangs of the past banded together for the purpose of survival and solidarity. Their familiarity was in their plight. They realized that together, they could do real things that would affect the real world. Their sense of identity was revealed through their unity. In unison, they could build a system that would support and protect them. Before the corruption of greed, there was a brotherhood; an era of oppression-bred resistance. Remember, historically, some of the greatest oppressors have bore the some of the greatest dissidents. Not to say that our government or police are tyrants, but in those times, racism, hatred, and sexism were bolder. The ancestral stories of blacks were still a heated pastime and coupled with a seemingly intolerable agreement, whites did not know what to expect from blacks. This fear continues to separate us. And although we may have a black president, we continue to trip ourselves up over politically correct terminology. And this divide is passed down through our parents understanding. These accounts fueled the gangs into racial unification. Initially, that was their unique bond—survival, race and family. But, as with time, ideas and motives are reorganized. Money, drugs, and power dissipated the original "honor" code. Today, gang members are killing their same affiliated members. I really see no purpose in calling yourself by any of the traditional gang names because you have so many crossovers that they are confusing each other. There is no tangible scene of structure, no loyalty, and definitely no love; only an out-of-control system that is driven by entertainment, drugs, and money.

There was a time when I held a position within the gang. At 17, I was considered an "officer". I was obsessed with gangbanging and those that were not, I felt were unworthy. Once, I was so upset with the boys that were under me that I'd threatened to abandon them. As I strolled off, one of the younger members (about 14) followed me and he began to cry. I looked at him and he said something to me that continues to hurt my heart. He said "I want to be like you" and he pledged his loyalty to me. I was terrible at this position in my life. I knew then what kind of influence that I held. I look back and if that is what he wanted to be like, then that was definitely a problem. But that is my point. We look to others for that sense of guidance. The sad part is that I was his peer and corrupt as I was, he admired me. Corrupt ideals are receptive in these environments. They are bred and nurtured in others to continue in the absence of the teacher. If the student finds fault in the teachings, he will not abandon them entirely, but will build upon the parts that have been successful to him. What I taught was wrong. I am sure that he in turn taught someone else. I have to take responsibility for that because I had the opportunity to guide him appropriately, but I didn't. When you have their attention, you have their loyalty.

When I was first initiated, I believed in the vision of the gang. You learn to believe in the cause and trust in the leaders. Their tactics were easy. We were us and everyone else was the enemy. Our goal was to make money and live lavishly. The particular gang that I was with incorporated Islamic teachings to make it seem as though we had a greater service to perform. It was all a ruse of course; just another attachment to keep us blinded by a purpose. They were articulate in their manipulation. It worked. Everything that we did was for the benefit of the "nation". As you grow up and perform more duties, you begin to realize that there are subgroups within the whole. These cliques are just the guys that have more in common, whether it is violence, notoriety, or the ambition to obtain more money. Whatever it is, you become more biased when it comes to the guys in your clique. You will go against others in the group for your closest friends. These immediate members are the ones that really hold power over each other. Years ago, personal cliquing was not acceptable. Everyone was responsible for everyone else. Today, high ranking members are judged by popular vote or monetary value. They can introduce any rules that they will benefit from. They may have no leadership skills but their wealth allots them their power. That leads to more disastrous problems for the subordinates. Looking on it now, this is one of the funnier paradoxes that I remember. As a teen, you don't want to be told what to do. You become rebellious because you don't want to listen. Yet, when you enter the streets, you are governed by those people and their rules. You are provoked to do things that you would not normally do. You end up serving a tyrant when that is what you thought you were fleeing from. Only in this case, you cannot walk away from them. Your parents may tolerate your temper. The streets will not.

I call us corruptors because that is exactly what we did. We deceived others into believing our lies. Once you become conscious that it is about your survival within the ranks, the sanctity of brotherhood is a joke. Leaders use subordinates to protect their interests. I've watched "Generals" force "soldiers" to do some deprecating things. I've seen boys put on roofs and in hallways to protect personal drug stores. I've even known leaders to use their power to take advantage of these subordinates sexually, in and out of prison, and not just girls. The subordinates are not in control. In the streets, there is always another in control of what you do. That is how they manipulate. They trick these teens into believing that they will be independent and have lavish freedom to do whatever they want, but in truth, they become enslaved to their leaders. If you are told to do something, you do it, or you will suffer for it. Adults always think that you have a choice or that no one put a gun to your head to make you do it. Well, once in this lifestyle, there does not need to be a gun to your head to know that if you defy the leadership, they could kill you.

Parents, teachers, and police all become the enemy because they are against the ideals of your crew. They don't understand the fight. Common sense, right? This separation is enforced the more you press your children about their social habits. Now, any request or inquiry is seen as antagonistic and will be refuted with belligerence. You now become part of the competition. They cannot trust you nor do they adhere to your warnings. The gang is now the safe haven. Where the leaders point, they will go. Their bond becomes stronger, and worse, your child becomes non-responsive to you. It is more effective if the child is already rebellious before he meets the gang.

They use false ideologies to sway these kids. Some use racial identity to forge a bond, which really works well if racism is a part of the community structure. If the teens are taught in the household not to trust another hue of people for whatever reason, they will band together and target those people. And why not make some money while you're committing crimes. These kids are reinforcing these ideas to each other. Taking out the leadership is essential, but without anything to substitute the hollowness, the other members will simply spread out. The leaders, horrible and incorrigible as they were, kept a certain amount of restraint on the members. You could not do whatever you wanted because it would fall back on the organization. Fear kept them in order. Respect and consequences held their attention. Without that structure, it is like being left alone at home for the first time. No parents and you feel a freedom from scrutiny. You feel as though you can get away with anything. Accelerate that by 20 times and you get pure mayhem.

Today's gangs are focused solely on their monetary gains. There is no brotherly pride in these mobs anymore. Since brotherhood and loyalty has been proven to be destroyed by greed, it is only natural for survival to kick in and they begin to descent into solitary corruption. In this state, they care about no one and will use or kill anyone that they believe is a threat.

Corrupt police keep the cycle of violence going as well. People in the community have no real idea about the law, which is why so many are caught up when something happens. There are plenty of corrupt officers and officials (recent years has revealed this), but there are good ones and you need to support them. They can get burned out if they feel as though they are alone. The good officers don't just make arrest. They actually try to understand the youth and their problems. They talk to you and are relentless. They become familiar with you and stay in range of you. We saw it as harassment but they were concerned, not just for the people that were law-abiding, but for us as well- the bangers. They need help. They cannot do it alone either.

The bad officers are the ones that beat these kids and take their money but not the drugs; the ones that confuse brutality with enforcement. These officers only see their jobs as simply a numbers system as opposed to a deterrent. Beating on these kids won't stop them. It only enforces what their leaders are telling them. Police are the enemy. This soon turns into a passionate hatred for them and you don't see them as people, but a target. You take away their humanity and they are easier to kill.

Neighborhoods must understand that you must truly support those that have your interest as a priority. Do your officers identify with you? Make them known and introduce them to your children. Personal relationships will be more effective. Don't force your children to believe that they are the enemy. Provocation goes both ways. Stop hiding in the shadows. Encourage your neighbors to sit out on your porches. Bangers don't want to do crimes in front of people. Too much activity makes them think too much. It's confusing. Don't hide and wait for them to commit a crime. Let them know that you are there and watching to prevent a crime from being committed. I don't care how much they may contribute to an area; they are still the poison that inflicts it. Gangs are a system and we must use a different schematic to impede this system. Your officers can pin down the gangs only so far, which is why you and your neighbors must produce a positive outlet that will inspire them.

Remember, the corruptors have a direct line to the youth. They have a bond with them. You must break this grip. You must untangle the hold that they have. This is not impossible. It just takes your dedication to your family. Use their logic to destroy the lie that the streets have told. Use reasoning to crack that deceptive image. It is a hoax. It is only attractive because we allow it to be. We give power to it by believing in its authority. Take back control in the life of your child because they certainly do not have it or they would not have given it away so freely. They need you and they don't know it. They require you to be strong for them. Do not wait for them to get so far off track that you don't recognize them anymore. Do something now. Be the enforcer, or would you rather the gang enforce them? If the neighborhood is unsafe, make them understand why. Don't just tell them, show them. Show them what real death looks like. Not like some movie or song. Take them to a cemetery, a hospital, or drive by a prison and ask them is that where they would like to spend the rest of their time at. Make it real for them, not some fantasy.

Prison is definitely not like in the movies and I'll tell you this, I bet all of the gang leaders that are incarcerated that will never see the outside again wish that they would have never started any of this mess. They would never have given away theirs or their family's life away so easily. Trust me, they do regret it; especially the ones that were betrayed by their own soldiers. The effect of something put into motion 40 or 50 years ago cannot be allowed to continue robbing us of our children today. If we do not take a stand now, there will be a scarcity of children for the future. I am from Chicago, this is not extreme; it is reality.

I get tired of hearing the same cliché "I don't want my children to have to go through what I went through", or "I want a better life for them". Apparently not, because we continue to promote the cesspool that we grew up in as if it defines our greatness. Many of us had the opportunity to do something different. We chose wrongly. No more excuses. No more worthless words that we believe sound justified.

Corruptors are only as effective as the people that they have control over. They have no real authority. Do not give them or their false ideologies about life any more power. Their wealth is more convincing than their words. Cripple their wealth and you cripple their power. Change the scene. Make them look like the enemy. If these entertainers are sincere in their desire to change the environment that they were born in, then they will help change the image of the streets. They cannot make it sound glorious to go to jail. Selling drugs and violence are not beneficial.

Do not allow drug dealers and gangs to take anything away from you. Take away from them what they have already stolen or attempted to steal from you, your life (your child). Your child is your life and if robbed of them, will you not truly be sickened in health due to the loss? Do not fear them nor submit. You were born an intelligent thinking being designed after the Creator of the earth. Do not permit your lineage to be destroyed by whatever you call this evil in the world. You have real power. Contrary to what people think, it is more difficult to do evil than to do good, especially when you know that the world is watching. If they know that you are not paying attention that makes it easier for them to prey. Stand firm in your position and do not allow them room to perform. They are the real terrorists; the monsters next door. They should fear you; you don't break the law. You are not the person that is going contrary to society. Do you know how some drug dealers and murderers stay alive for so long? Because they are some of the most paranoid people on the planet. When they know that something is not right, they don't act. When there is too much attention, they back off. Fear of prison or death keeps the upper ranks from making the common mistakes that their subordinates make. But know that just decapitating the leadership won't stop the cycle. To keep others from popping up, a system must be put into position. Not a system designed by people that have no experience or personal interest; a system that does not fail just because one or two people do. That is why a community must come together with law-enforcement, business people, and the working class. Change the perspective of what is required of men and women. Our culture envelops us with the ideals of having everything that gives us pleasure. Do not just hope that your children will not fall into the sway of these people.

When you have economic and social poverty, historical tension, and racial disunity, you have a melting pot for chaos. And these cannot be attributed to one hue of people. Whites cannot be blamed for all of black's problems just as blacks cannot be blamed for all of white's problems. These ideals are passed down and evolve just as a virus does. There are still problems in certain places but it is just not tolerated as it once had been. Although you may see police brutality in the news, every officer is not out to terrorize these areas. People get tired of seeing children hurt and killed. I have been beat up by cops but I know that had I not been in the streets acting up, the chances of them hurting me would not have been as great. I understand how frustrating it is when you see someone doing something so totally idiotic that you just want to scream. You wonder, what the hell could they be thinking? Some of the things that these gangs say today amazes me because they make no sense or they are the same quotes from 20 years ago that sound dumb today just as they did then. It is if the garbage is simply being regurgitated.

Want to hear something ridiculous? Guess what the foundation is that most gangs promote? Knowledge, wisdom, understanding, truth, loyalty, freedom, life, peace, justice, and love. Yes, I'm serious. But they really do not practice these ideals. They look nice when you get a tattoo but they are not applied. The only smart guys are the ones that learn how to manipulate, stay out of jail, and continue to make money while others take the fall. The new generations are just being deceived with old ideas covered with new words. It equals bull.

You want to hear something incontestably hilarious? This whole *stop snitchin'* campaign. All of the street guys are upset about people about turning their butts in but many of the so-called "titans" that we idolized are stool pigeons. The guy on top in many cases is the same one to take everyone else down. He gets the most pressure. Look at Frank Lucas in New York. That is reality. The guy with all of the blood on his hands makes the deals with the state or feds. Corruptors are disgusted with people that work with the police yet law enforcement would not be as effective if there was not a breach within criminality. A lot of times these guys simply talk too much and tell on themselves. They think that coming up with codes and clues will work. When you are being watched and recorded, how long do you really believe that it will be before that code is cracked? These guys get arrogant and believe that they cannot be touched. They fail to learn from history. Look at the Italian mobs; very strong and powerful at one point and desecrated by some of the top commanders. The Japanese Yakuza, one of the most disciplined and feared, even have their defectors. The Mexican mafia, renowned for its brutality, still has their informants. Escobar owned Columbia, but when the people got tired and fought back, he was killed. There are people within these settings that will only go so far. They signed up for the profit, not the bloodshed. You also have natural monsters that just enjoy what they do.

Every time one of these entertainers goes on T.V. and proclaims to sell drugs in certain areas, on specific blocks, or in airplanes or boats, they are telling. What? Do they think that law enforcement does not pay attention? The idiots that flash their guns and drugs on T.V. show the exact locations of their spots (hiding places) and are the real informants. They tell the world, "Hey, I'm right here!"

Their hood, their homeboys; that love. You'll hear this frequently expressed by some of these teens but what they are really looking for is to fit in with what they believe to be success. Their parents and family are not always negligent. All of these teens do not come from a home filled with chaos. So what are they really missing? Acceptance within themselves and their peers; that need to feel wanted is deep and exciting. It feels purposeful.

Corrupt ideals are inherited throughout generations. The same parents that want better for their children (with a criminal lifestyle) are the same ones that infected them with offset ethics. Children watch intently. If you commit crimes to provide for that child, they learn and absorb it. Even that child's friends learn from this. They consider them the cool parents. Now, a child has been taught to go through exactly what that parent has gone through. Even in middle income households, when a parent is always working, the child learns that working for money is necessary but being a slave to it is depressing. How do they avoid the chains of servitude? Drugs. But drugs are actually a more fervent form of slavery to money. The risk is too great. It is a path that binds us in death and justifies our happiness. That is why the appeal of that path must be broken. This deceptive position must be challenged on a massive scene.

I want to clarify something about a very controversial term. The term "nigga" is frequented by many generations of people in that lifestyle. Many adults use it as well so teens are not the only ones in error for this terrible usage. Of course they say that they have changed its meaning. The word nigga is not and will never be a term of endearment. They can mask it any way that they choose to, but it is still derogatory. Some attempt to say that it expresses camaraderie. What a joke! When you are referring to a friend, most of the time you will say, "This is my boy, my guy, my homie, or my dog". Ninety percent of the time when the term nigga is used, it is in reference to an enemy. It is frequently used out of anger, frustration, or when referring to others that you have no concern for. You could never take this word and use it in a glorifying manner. They even try to say that when other people use it, it simply means an ignorant person. That is because they are ignorant (unaware or have no understanding) in what they are saying. That is like me saying, "Oh a slut is not a bad thing, it just means strong ladies uniting truth". It just means that you like sex. What woman would look at this word as alluring or appealing? The term nigga is menacing. Everyone that I know that has used it meant disrespect when they spewed it out of their mouths. It is a venomous word that can never be stripped of its evil connotation. We have just adopted it while accepting it. This is just another way to continue the justification of a depraved mind. We must stop telling these kids not to follow in "my path". It never was "our path", but a path forged long ago for a non-existent purpose that continues to repeat itself. No matter how many grammatical surgeries that this word takes, it will never be a term of endearment nor its meaning changed.

Why Are We Responsible? Redemption

With the tremendous direction that the country is moving in, people are asking the question, "Can people really change?" It needs to be understood that change deals with a choice. It is not simply one step or decision. It is not as simple as our imaginations would like for us to believe. We want people to make different choices but we sometimes dupe ourselves. People will always be intertwined with what they have experienced, good or bad, but have they decided to choose a different strategy?

Change incorporates realizing that the choices that you act upon always affect someone else. Your choices are real and what you put out will be reciprocated. Change requires an attitude shift and a re-evaluation of ideas. Understanding that your attitude alone on a daily account affects other people's moods; mishandling a situation can be disheartening to someone else.

I, myself, have agreed to atone for the errors that I have made. Those people, that have forsaken the street life, the chaos, the depravity, are indebted to the balance of life. Due to our arrogance and our ignorance, we afflicted others. We are bound to this cause by our growth and our guilt. Our compassion for living acknowledges our mistakes and drives us to do better for the sake of redeeming ourselves in life. I know that just as I and others were deceived into the madness, we can also see the truth in the chaos and deter it.

How must we redeem ourselves? By putting in the same time, dedication, discipline, energy, and sacrifice that we placed into the negative aspect of our lives. It must now be put into a manner that benefits others in need of guidance. And it must prove to them our effectiveness. This requires sincerity and diligence due to the amount of harm that has already been caused.

The human mind incorporates so many thoughts. Some understood, some not so clear. We don't want to live in a world filled with hate, wickedness, and chaos. Yet, this is naiveté. God created a balance and right now, we are a part of that balance. Whether we believe in its fairness or genuineness is not ours to contest. It is our duty to perform our acts according to the parameters set forth. All things come from the mind, an idea, and they all dissipate back into that origin. What we must do is destroy a bad idea with a better idea. Before the bad idea can be fully entertained, the good idea must be more persuasive. All gangs began with an idea and can be destroyed by a better system.

Why are we responsible? Because anyone that believes in a Divine Creator is bound to humanity. Anyone that says that they believe in the Bible, Qu'ran, Taoism, etc., is bound by its instructions.

The prophet Ezekiel was made a watchman over Israel. They were his duty, his people. He spoke their language. Afflicted people have a language to. It is called suffering and it has no borders. Anyone in the world can speak it if you have experienced it. If you speak their language, they will be more receptive. Those of us that have now accepted life and understand it still speak their language. But we can now speak the truth of life in their language. Those that have escaped the grasp of that lifestyle are in the most pivotal position to pull others out. The Scriptures tell us that we must save those that are leaning towards death (Proverbs 24: 11-12). Those that are following after a disastrous trend must be proven the error in it. Their lifestyle is killing them and they think that they are fully aware of it. They are trapped by it and cannot even see it. And if they are aware of it, they are afraid to depart from it. If you see someone that is about to be hit by a car, do you stand there and watch? Of course not! You yell and scream to get their attention. We have become so selfish in our lives that it is a wonder that we are not consuming each other literally.

Everyone needs atonement. Everyone must be redeemed for something. Albeit to us, some things appear worse than others, and unforgiveable, that is a human thought. It is an understandable feeling when you have suffered unnecessarily.

Is our society getting worse or are we allowing it to? Our world is more interconnected today than before. We see the atrocities committed and wonder why someone would do what they have done. These are not new criminal ideas, only refined.

Do we really believe that we could forgive someone that did harm to us or our family? Because of someone's crimes in the past, does that negate their obligation to help others? Especially, if it may benefit another's life? The people that have died and those that have suffered deserve something more. The people that have died due to violence cannot be allowed to have died for a statistic. Just as their life had purpose, so must their death. Their lives are now intertwined with ours. Our lives must be in service to humanity. Those that have died must cause others to live. That is the balance. That is the cycle. That is the duty of one who has taken responsibility and desires atonement. This is how life endures. Whether you guide your children, your neighbor's children, or a child in the streets, you must cause that spark.

Many of us turned away from God. We trusted in our money, our guns, and in our associates. We turned our backs because we did not understand God. In one facet, it appeared to be another form of oppression, in another, it was a scapegoat, because you could do whatever you wanted and be forgiven. You could be bad and still have time to do right and get into heaven. In our youth, we could not truly conceptualize the identity or purpose of God. This provided opportunity for us to fall deeper into corruption.

If a person desires repentance, then they must first introspect (look at who they are and where they would like to be), retrospect (remember their past and never forget those errors, as to not make them again), and extrapolate (appreciate who they are and build on the person that they are). To recover from the sins of our past we must be strategic, systematic, passionate, and driven. You want to be a better person? Build on the best parts of you while shaving off the worst.

I hear people say that they are not ashamed of anything that they have done. This is a problem. Shame (in certain instances) keeps you from committing certain acts. It is that shame for bad elements that stop you from doing them. If you are not ashamed of something, then you will freely do it without competence or circumspection. It becomes natural the more that you practice it. Activity in the streets must be seen as shameful. Drug dealing, gangbanging, shooting must be turned into shameful, unacceptable acts, by all people. You don't protect your child by covering up the bad things that they do. You are not helping them by not invading their privacy. Saving them requires that you stand in their way when they are walking towards a cliff. Learn from those that have already fallen. Use those of us that have crashed in our lives.

I want to talk about this no snitching campaign. It amazes me that the same people that want the telling to stop are the same people committing the crimes. What position does a rapper really have against it if he is making money legitimately? Why would it even bother them if they are not in the criminal element? One thing that is very clear to me now is that I have no fear of law enforcement because I do not involve myself with the things that will give them reason to bother me. I am not naive to believe that there are no corrupt officers, but there is not a great proportion of the time when a cop will just harass you. Maybe if we were not standing on the corners looking as if we were up to something they would not have bothered us. Maybe if we did not hang out in known drug spots they could not have put drugs on us. It is not always the police who put drugs on people, sometimes you really are at the spot when you should not be, and that is the key, not being in the area where you know that there is a possible risk for trouble. Again, there are unjustifiable harassments and abuses within the police departments, but if you are not a criminal, why would you be worried about someone telling on you?

The truth is what matters. Truth will bind us together and hypocrisy will destroy that bond. Liars can tell some fantastically fantastic stories. We must stop giving credence to them. Those that are looking to redeem themselves are willing to sacrifice to achieve the necessary results. It is far more difficult to continue on the road burdened by corruption, although the path of redemption is not so golden either. The difference is that this path will cleanse you in the eyes of people and God. This journey will allow you peace. It will shed the pains of incurred tragedy. Meaning the incidents that we placed upon ourselves will be relieved from us.

Being redeemed means becoming employed. You serve a new purpose. You have a new job and a new life. You are bound to your decision. Seeking redemption requires seeking a commitment. Look at the stock market. When you buy shares, you are looking for a great deal which means that you are looking to purchase a stock for a low price in the event that it will rise in the future. You don't just purchase because the price is cheap. You view its overall potential and possible future earnings. Ironically, cashing in on your shares is called "redeeming". A person must become like this. At the point of return, they must be a worthy investment to become redeemed. People that have committed crimes against society have lost their value. The share price has dropped. One day, they will be called to see if the price is redeemable and if not, that investment will be considered a loss.

I know that it seems as though every time that we look at the T.V., there is another crime committed by another parolee or ex-con. It almost seems like, "Why bother to give these people another chance when they'll just hurt someone else?" Society could easily say that they never want to let anyone out of prison. Commit a crime; go to jail for life; no appeal; no pleas. Do you really believe though that this would deter crime? No, I don't think so. It seems as though when we see the horrendous fall of which a human can plummet, it sparks others to be that much better. It is sad to see how badly that we can treat one another but to see just how great we can be to one another enforces that there is a need in the world for forgiveness.

Redemption requires us to recover what we lost. We must obtain the part of our life that we threw away. Our past must not be allowed to destroy our future, and to do this requires dedication. Society does not need meaningless words but transparent action.

I believe that friendships and connections are forged in 3 parts; Commonality, sincerity, and comfortability.

I think that there must be first common goals, ideas, and burdens that bring people together. There has to be a struggle that links people for there to be openness. This is true for those trying to correct their errors in the face of others. People will naturally move towards those that share similar problems or dreams. This also helps you believe in a person's sincerity because when there are common interests, you know that they are affected as well.

Sincerity is a strong but proof related factor. It can not only be seen but felt as well. You can literally feel a person's spirit when they are filled with passion. Their sincerity is revealed through their eyes and actions. People looking to be redeemed, to reconcile for past discrepancies, must live through compassion. Real guilt, real understanding for wrongdoing, will drive a person to continuously work through selfishness.

Comfortability requires you to allow people to express themselves with you. When people are comfortable, they show the truth of who they are. They trust you and find security within you. If you have wronged in the past, let it stay there. Redemption needs for you to pay back that debt. That space must be filled. Comfortability brings out happiness because a person does not need to fear ridicule or deprecation. This is something that our kids face on a drastic level.

To recognize guidelines and to live in them takes courage; it takes strength to say "I was wrong and forgive me". Everyone seeks everyday to redeem themselves from their past errors, whether they acknowledge it or not. You don't know who you may have harmed indirectly from reckless behavior. That is why service is so critical. Humans recognize tangible actions. We want to believe in the good of people's words, the genuineness of their inspiration, but if they are not striving to live, then there will be suspicions.

Those that seek forgiveness and redemption must be appreciative of the opportunity given. If they are grateful then the lives of others will hold great value to them. Their selfish ideas will no longer command their decisions. In redeeming themselves, they recognize the errors that they have acted upon and now seek feasible ways of correcting them. Even when people say "gangs are forever", those seeking redemption knows that this is not true. They know that the lies being taught can be overthrown by the truth of life. Responsibility is accepted by those that choose to change.

Someone has to accept responsibility. Someone must recognize that their errors caused a rippling effect. Accepting responsibility does not condemn us but allows us to correct the effects of the past. If no one ever says, "I caused this or it is my fault", how will we ever know where the rupture happened? We must stop using scapegoats and deniability to justify our mistakes. You can't just walk away from your transgressions. They must be amended and then you move forward.

Inspiring A Generation: Persuasion and Influence

The most violent children are so because they are immersed in the script. They no longer desire to turn it off. They enjoy the ruthlessness that they cause. These are the ones that are really broken. The children whose parents are on drugs or sell drugs obviously teach us where their encouragement comes from. But that does not mean that it is established either; they can be dissuaded as well. Not your problem? Yes, it is. Simply telling your children not to befriend someone from that element does not necessarily stir deterrence. Get involved by helping your children's friends. Show them the difference in the world. Expose the false limitations placed on them by their surroundings.

Those of us that grow out of these roles either become smarter within our fields (selling drugs, guns, etc.) or we move away from that lifestyle looking for another avenue. Not all gangs require you to get beat out or death as a resignation. If you are indeed attempting to be an upright person, there are leaders that have and will express encouragement with that decision, but you must be sincere. A man I knew was in prison and decided to step away from the gang life. He thought that initially he would be afraid, alone, a traitor. He didn't know what to expect and if any old enemies would attack him. He had to take the chance though. He had to believe enough in himself to step away from what he had known. He had encouragement from his fellow members that wanted to do the same but lacked the ambition to do so. He also sought guidance from those that had done what he was about to do. Some people will read this and say that you cannot inspire someone out of bad behavior. Well, if fear of death and incarceration does not deter them from the insanity, what will? Some people think that the youth are too far into their corruption and can't be saved. See, I have a problem with that because I believe in a Creator that has designed apt beings with the option of choices. Divine inspiration through a human being cannot be equaled with monetary or material accruements. I do not care who you are or where you are, if we are to help the youth get back to life, then we must make sure that we, ourselves, are in a position to do so. Understand, that they are watching you and if you are hypocritical in your dealings or words, then how can you expect for them to be any different? Their faith in life (and in you) will be shattered. This confuses their trust in everyone.

I realize that some of you may think that this has nothing to do with you; that your children are safe. Well, analyze this idea, who is your child (or neighbors child) talking to when you are not around? Who are they sharing ideas with? Who are they admiring? It does not have to be about your career status or wealth, information is everywhere and so easily available, and villainous actions are hailed as cool. Let me give you a little clarity. Look at the names that these kids invoke. The names and characters that they mimic, Gotti, Capone, Nitti, Noriega, and so forth, are known criminals and they are admired for their dissidence. We glorify them for their remarkable achievements in the criminal climate. I have no doubt that had any of these men chose a different field in life, they could have been great business leaders, but the fact is that they were criminals. Just as those that attempt to be like them are criminals. Following in their paths is not heroic or defining. The idea of rebellion is just exciting. Living and worrying about nothing, making decisions on site is shocking. That is the illusion. No consequences. No concept of punishment. No thought of anything logical.

In this lifestyle, you copycat those that precede you and you actually believe that you will be different. Greater because you think that you are smarter or more advanced than the generation before you. You won't make their mistakes. No, not you because they were not as sharp or don't have the technology that you have. Selling drugs was probably one of the most difficult "jobs" that I have seen. Although the payout can be enormous, the market risk is very high. There is no FDIC or SIPC to protect your savings and invest-ments. Why do you think that drug dealers are so paranoid? There's no insurance. Consider these factors.

The Police are enemy number one because their entire duty is to stop you. They can take everything away from you legally. They are the largest opposition that you must protect yourself from because they can destroy you monetarily and physically.

Other drug dealers; the competition is always there. This creates more stress because you have to work long hours to make sure that the product is bigger in size or better in substance, and that you don't run out when you have customers.

Stick-up men; these are the guys that will kill you for the money or the dope. They are everywhere and can be anyone. The good thing is that sometimes they are so clumsy or obvious that you recognize them before they get to you.

The Clientele, of course, anyone that is shopping will be looking for a good deal but people that are addicted to drugs are the best when it comes to bargaining. They will attempt any ploy to get what they want at the cheapest price.

Yourself; People that have not had a lot of money before sometimes become overwhelmed when they receive it. It makes them feel free from the restraints that poverty, ridicule, and uncertainty has placed on them. You can actually become addicted to counting money. It becomes more than just about surviving. It evolves into a quest about being on top of everybody.

These kids think that if they are neighborhood celebrities then their life will matter. They believe that if they can be someone admired, their life will be whole and happy. Many teens are duped by this belief. They do not even consider the ratio. The few that had lived the lifestyle for thirty years solidified to us that it could be done. We never even looked at the 90% that had failed and fallen. Those that had died lived on in legend.

We were inspired. I know the look of inspiration and the feeling of motivation. I admired my leaders and wanted to make them, as well as my friends, proud of me. I wanted to prove my sincerity and my conviction to them.

I totally believe in the power of influence. Responsibility must be accepted on all fronts. These rappers can say what they want and while I agree that music cannot force you to do anything, technically, neither can Satan. I mean, the devil, really does not force us to harm one another but Satan does encourage you. I am not calling rap or rappers the devil either. And although we do not hold people responsible too much for what they say, the words that they put out do influence you. There were times when I and my friends did not have the courage to act out (although we would not admit it), we would listen to someone with more "experience" to boast our assurance. Music has a way of encouraging you to believe in things, people, and ideas. Music in the past has been used to rally and stir up soldiers before and during a battle. Certain sounds can have an emotional effect on us and while I have no scientific data to prove this, I have seen enough kids influenced to do stupid things under the guise of coolness. When you are continuously admonished that shooting people is how problems are corrected, you believe this. Ever notice how these kids can't tell you about current issues but they can recite an entire album verbatim. So what do you think that their minds are on? You or their idols? Believe me; you may not hold the authority that you may think that you do. If people do not collectively work together to curve the persuasion of these teens, they may take their entire generation (and the one that follows) to the grave with them in the name of infamy.

Just as gang leaders held our attention, civilized people must take control of that focus. How do you get their attention? By taking the responsibility of directing their inspiration. Our words must be succeeded by direct actions. Their recklessness must be dissipated by empirical understanding. If we show them why something is erroneous as opposed to hiding it from them, they will be more receptive to understanding why we want them to avoid it. To earn their loyalty, our results must be proven. We must be disciplined and show them how to be progressive. It must be understood that they are easily persuaded and their idols are actors themselves in the entertainment world. It is time to shake up this platform.

If we do not have anything to offer them that is more stimulating than the persuasion of their lifestyles, we will fail. The truth of their so-called leaders must be revealed. The treachery of their brotherhood must be shown in order for them to see the carelessness of their lives. The force of the gang's structure may not be as paramount but the gravity of the lifestyle does not shift because of a gang's failure to adapt or grow. Most of the original founders are either dead or incarcerated, but their ideologies are still evident today. The street lifestyle is not limited to any one gang, which is why you have so many cliques with opposite gang members. These hybrid groups share a commonality that is deeper than the gang's influence. Realizing that war in the streets does not keep you fed allows you to put some of your conflictions to the side. This is a small step into their reasoning. This small opening allows for a different view to become inserted into their lives. But it is also dangerous because it exposes the gang's weakness. If members don't respect their own codes, then they are more encouraged to be violent. Rules and fear of breaking them kept gangs in order. If they are not in order with their rules, they become equivalent to mercenaries.

We must remember that language is still a great barrier between people. We, as an American Democracy, cannot allow our language to divide us. No matter the particulars, to communicate effectively, we must understand their language. Not so much in their literal jargon, but in the way in which they inspire each other, motivates one another, and leads one another in their everyday endeavors. Young people are influenced more by what they see. Their eyes are sharper than their perception. We must become what they need. Not simply in speech or idea, but we must be the leaders that they feed from.

Deliverers were used in times past to get the people safely out of a harmful condition to a safer plateau. These deliverers understood the conditions of the people that they were aiding and they performed the services needed to benefit the community.

In order to save these children, these misdirected teens, we must be willing to proceed with sincere intentions. The gap must be closed between adults and their children. No communication is severely dangerous. Adults must be humbled and patient. The youth are easily antagonized and with so much fire breathing through them, over the top emotions only push them further into depravity. Don't become the enemy because you don't understand. Understand their position but make sure that they understand yours. If you see the danger, show it to them before they fall into the trap. You don't want that call that your child is dead or in jail for something heinous. Save your child by not just being involved in their lives but their friends as well.

I don't want this to appear as some sort of point program as those done in the past. The following are just some ideas that I and fellow ex-members recognize as things that can be implemented to have an impact. Some of these ideas may already be in action but they must be focused at holding their attention. They must be able to relate to the idea as well as the person applying it.

We must be successful. If we have nothing to offer them, they will not be attentive.

Find out what they are truly passionate about. Encourage it and inspire them with real assistance. Build upon it with them so that they will believe in it.

We must be articulate and persuasive but not foreign in our language. Struggling for their minds will take influence.

We must fill in that void that this boredom and idleness creates. When they have nothing on their itinerary, they hang out and find trouble.

To keep our work from warping later on, our foundation must be able to evolve and absorb the shocks of an ever changing world.

They must be shown the value of their lives and what they mean to this world. Help them understand the world that they live in.

They seek attention, and they must receive it through active bonding, mainly through activities that build their trust in one another. Loyalty is earned through their experience with someone.

They must see civil adults as a real power, a credible hierarchy worthy of their respect. This is how they view the entertainment world. Those are their selected leaders.

We must be precise and to the point. If our direction or actions are drawn out and unclear, they will grow tired of aimless wandering.

Our communities are at war and we must analyze exactly what

it is that we have passed on. Look at the way we have chosen to interact with ourselves, our children, and each other. Has the human element been subtracted from our relationships? E-mail, Texting, twittering; busy, busy, busy. Have we become that negligent? Yes, we have. The children in all communities are learning simply from T.V. or the Internet. Unguarded, they become fascinated by the forbidden things that they are uneducated to.

There are plenty of real heroes and idols. They should not be limited to T.V. The adult, the civil adult, has to become the hero again. The entrepreneur, the laborer, and the civil servant must be seen as heroes.

I know that working at a young age has a long term effect upon you. It amazes me sometimes that the things instilled in you in your youth are a part of your everyday activities, even unconsciously. We are influenced by our peers and whether it is right or wrong, the power of their view towards us sometimes outweighs our reason, especially when we are young. Children are also inspired by adults, but they are watching their peers more intently. The same is valid for young adults. Of course, there are those in crowds and they hold their own exclusive rights. There's not too much damage in that until the crowd hold only themselves in authority.

Everyone that becomes a part of the streets takes on a role. Look at the screenplay. Everyone is an actor except here you design your character. Some of us were not violent or bad children, but the qualifications of our position required us to be so. You create the character so that shields the real you. It protects you from being seen as weak or cowardly. Some of us grow out of these roles and some of us grow deeper in. Those that become one with their roles are the ones that you see have no concern for life. There are others that gave up that entire lifestyle. He had to give up that entire way of thinking. His language was changed as well as the way he interacted with people. Surprisingly, he felt relieved. A burden had been taken away. He was not bound to someone else's idea of right and wrong. He was not forced to fight for some reason unknown to him. He was, in effect, Free. The funny thing was that all while he was affiliated, he thought that his enemies were the opposite gangs, but once he separated himself, he found himself becoming close friends with the same men that he was told were his enemies.

The power of influence will turn children against parents, siblings against each other, and a person against himself. Are you getting it? Your children are not safe simply because you do not live in a bad neighborhood. Because you do not allow them to listen to rap music or because you just know your child. Most parents believe that they know their children and are awestruck at what they are capable of doing. Look at the string of shootings in Chicago by children. Don't you think that those parents knew their children? Or do you want to believe that those were simply low-income, irresponsible, negligent parents? Here's a tip: Ask your children who is the realest rapper today? Ask them do they know who has been to jail? If they can answer this question for you, then they know something of the street life, if only vicariously through the music or movies. And I am not saying that the music alone will make them become gangsters but do not think that they are as unaware as they may seem.

Many people on this planet are familiar with the history of blacks being referred to by the term nigger. It was instituted as a point of control but that time has passed on. Now, it has taken on some plastic surgery and it is hailed as a general expression. The word has crossed over hue and neighborhoods. Anyone feeling poor, oppressed, or depressed identify with the term. They, in turn, assimilate more into the negative idea that it propagates. They think that to be a real "nigga" means to be tough, fearless, and have the credentials to prove it. Whites (in the street life) use this term just like the blacks and it is not seen as racist, just a word for reference to someone on the opposite side. As I spoke about earlier, it is not a term used to express friendship, but it is used to justify a position. A position that is considered oppressed which justifies a rebellious attitude. It justifies their oppressed thinking.

The influence can seem intoxicating. You can crave it. That is something that law enforcement cannot defeat; the compelling drive of the human spirit to do something. Intimidation only permeates so far, which is one reason why recidivism is so high. Fear works until the human ability to adapt takes control. And talking only works a short span and only if you hold their attention. Understand that there was a time when their rebellion had more justification. Police had a terrible image for brutal tactics as deterrence. They may have believed that fear would stop crime. But what they did was create a more dissident environment for the people that they had sworn to protect. And this created the opportunity for someone to make money off of the exploits of the suffering. Power is given to those that are admired; those that are seen as worthy of it. In the eyes of a teen, that person does not have to be responsible as long as they are alluring. Even adults admire those that are attractive and articulate in speech, savvy in character, or witty in response. Think about the people that you idolized. Although they may not have been violent, you were still enraptured by their presence. We are in an era when family morals are not as stringent as before. Freedom has taken a new course and has spiraled into a new direction with our values becoming blurred along the way. We still have laws that fail to catch up with technological advances. It took almost 10 years to uncover Bernie Madoff's scheme, if you aren't paying attention, then who is? You cannot ignore what you suspect. Trust me; you may save your child's life.

I, myself, have no children but I can tell you that it is easier to persuade a teen to do something crazy when the parent appears ignorant, then one that is constantly involved in their life. I understand that you want to trust your child, and you should, but you also need to be aware in the event that they need reinforcement. Influence your neighbor's child as well. Fortify their parent's good teachings. This could in turn save your child. Negligence in a community only births recklessness. They are not in control and adults are so busy that they cannot see. Get involved and let them feel your involvement. Don't tolerate the silence, the secrecy, or the tantrums. They live in your home. They are temporarily occupying space. It is your duty to protect them. Even if they are upset with you for some time, at least they will live. If you feel as though you need to intervene, do it. Prison is full of men whom were guided by their friends. I understand that people do react to their environment and sometimes they are a result of it, but it cannot be the main factor that determines who they will become. You must be that pivotal factor. So change the circumstances in the environment. Change the mind, the structure, and the status simultaneously. If the mental platform is changed, then more people will get involved. As they watch it evolve, they too will advance. The people will interact with more solidarity. A new direction must be set. Our children are more advanced and conscious of us then we are of them.

Anyone can be influential. Anyone can become an idol. We must work together to show these teens that real heroes, real idols live right in their neighborhoods; maybe within their own households. Be who they desire to become. Inspire them by being seen as a renowned person. No matter your occupation, people can see the energy that dwells within you, and so can your children. Use it to guide them; to attract them to you or another positive entity. Experience teaches but it cannot be the only lesson. They must learn from people that share the same plight.

Pay attention to your children. Making the things in their life seem small really hurts them and they won't forget it. If you neglect them, there is always someone else that won't. The power of pride that your child will feel in knowing that what they do is important to you is very effective in their everyday decisions—that what they say and think really matters in life. Give your child the chance to show you who they are, and appreciate them for it. This will enforce their desire to be better.

Remember, there are some really bad people out there with a lot of influence and all of them are not criminals in the streets. Stay informed of what is going on inside of your home as well as outside. You are not by yourself. Seek out other parents that need your support, just as you need theirs. Form a network that will protect everyone. Get your children to watch out for each other and to alert someone when something is off. Take control to preserve your child's life or it will belong to another.

Influence has more power over them then some people would like to recognize. Just make sure that if you are not the most potent influence to them, that whatever it may be, it is a positive direction. Inspiring a generation will definitely require the spark of persuasion and the guidance of influence.

Inspiring A Generation Confidence

Inspiration is a power that can move in two directions. You can be inspired into evil, just as you can to do good. The effect of the inspiration depends upon the confidence already within the individual. Violence is inspired when there is a belief that it is for a greater objective. Soldiers kill the enemy to serve a country. Police kill criminals that are an immediate and deadly threat. Even martyrdom in religion is hailed as heroic. The same idea is applied in the streets. No one just wants to be violent (sorry, there are some wackos). Many of these kids think that this is how the streets work and so you are taught that if you are violent, no one will test you.

Confidence is required for them to stand against alluring influences. It must be earned and refined. Why is this an issue? Because if they are not confident in who they are, they will never be satisfied with what they do. They will face ridicule, opposition, and adversity and they must possess the courage to resist it or they will fall into the mayhem.

People lack confidence when they are unsure; when they don't know about something or what to do, and they become easily persuaded by someone that is more confident (or at least appears to be). Teens have no real experience, which is why some of them are so observant. You can learn how to drive a car by watching and mimicking. You study the speed, their hands on the wheel, and their eyes. When you sit behind the wheel, you feel the feeting arrangement and understand. You emulate what you see. The same is in the streets. The violence, the language, the characters, you replay.

Repetition builds confidence. Even when you fall, something pushes you to try it again. The youth must be assured that being confident in themselves, even when their friends are provoking them to do something stupid, is not cowardly. How do we do this? Give your child exercises to complete. Give them real world experience. Take them out and challenge them. Teach them how to be witty and smart. Do not assume that they know. Show them how to defend against ridicule. They may get bored quickly, so you must stay ahead of them. Humans adapt quickly and the youth are always actively searching for excitement.

Get your children to understand that what they do does affect the lives of other people. The sum of their actions will allow them to understand but you don't want them crashing in a lesson.

People do not always comprehend simply by hearing and seeing. Applying an idea to real life expresses assurance. It is a feeling that lets you know that you can make something happen in real life.

In your mistakes, you learn. They learn. Instead of letting them learn how to outmaneuver you, show them how to outsmart the troublemakers. Even when people fail at something, they see a result. This can also be used to build confidence. A mistake must be seen as a miscalculation, not a tragedy. Teach them how to be receptive to criticisms and advice. If they understand the possibilities of what could happen, then if something does go wrong, they won't be as distraught. This requires practice. Make it pleasing for them. They must learn (feel) to trust and build within themselves.

We must stop allowing a teen's look to decide their position in life. We know that looks play an important role to them because they express it. We see these distinctive characteristics in billboards, magazines, and T.V. Why shouldn't they feel as though they need to prove themselves? Masculinity is defined all around them.

No sign of weakness or sensitivity. It is taught to them by everything around them except you.

Our pride as men is a significant factor. Not that women are not prideful, it is just that males take pride and do some really irrational things in its name. As teens, we were rebellious due to the values that we were taught about manhood. Whether learned in the household or in the streets, boys will pick up on the attributes of who they see as a man. They will mimic it to the point where they feel confident enough to surpass it. If the person that they mimic has no concern for life, then this is of course dangerous. They will commit more elevated acts of hate and crime. They mature into it until it becomes logical. Our pride can blind us and have us believe in suspicions that are non-existent which is why violence is the first answer to their problems.

You believe that you can eliminate the fear, the anger, and the problem all in one manner.

Take the drug dealer for example. Many people sell drugs to survive. It's cheap, simple, and profitable. As they acquire more, they must sustain a particular lifestyle—a certain standard by which to live. They must account for possible errors and losses. Now if they were instructed to another avenue, another path which to maintain that void without backlash, I believe that more will be prone to success. Drug dealers sell the commodity that is in demand. They have price wars which can lead to gun wars. But what if you could eliminate the threat of death and danger from their endeavors? If more of these kids are introduced to real entrepreneurs and learn the inner workings of business, it will not only help the social perspective of that area but the economic as well.

The lack of confidence within these children is not their fault. We have not instilled them with defining perspectives. The average person born in this country cannot even define their inalienable rights (Life, liberty, and the pursuit of happiness). Why? Because we have become so comfortable that we neglect them. Their value is underscored by our influences. We always talk about freedom and democracy, yet we fail to protect our most important interest; our children. Their confidence is so limited. Do they really know what it means to be proud of who they are as a person? Show your children the value of working. Who cares what you do for a living. The point is that you are living. I think that every parent should give their child a ledger in which they should put down every penny received and spent. Teach them more than just the necessity of money. Show them how to appreciate money but not to overvalue it, which in the absence of, can lead to depression and irrationality. In the inner city, there are kids that think that economics deals with homecare. That just shows you how unaware that many teens are in the world that they are a part of. They are quite possibly naive to the real dangers in their midst. I meet young adults today that are unaware of the biggest topics in the news. They are not stupid, but they are uninterested, because they don't see how these things affect them. They cannot make the connection (especially between business and the entertainment world).

Consistent repetition of real information and knowledge is great but application of ideas is also needed in order for the feeling to fortify the drive. They feel fear, which is why they do not proceed further on, because they may face ridicule from their peers. They are not confident in their decisions, and they must be careful not to allow their confidence to turn into arrogance. Assure them of their ability by truly investing in them. Help them stay diligent in what they desire to do. You must build with them until they know that they can succeed in this endeavor. Telling them is great but getting involved excels them. If you, a person that is close to them, has no faith in them or their ideas, why should they? How do you think that they feel?

Negative confidence is when extremities are allowed to make their decisions. The affect that excitement has upon them is very strong. The music, the fame, builds confidence in them to continue in their treachery. History, environment, color, are continuous impediments that gangs use as excuses to promote their anarchal nature. People always seem to justify their improprieties with the cliché "it's a way of life". There are no multiple ways of life. There is life and there is death. The path that we choose will decide whether we live or die.

Confidence in the streets is built. I do not care who they are, everyone is scared their first time doing something illegal. As you continue on and get away with your crimes, you become more assure of yourself. The praise from your friends and the girls motivate you to contend more. It becomes exciting. You feel as though you have meaning because things are going on within your life.

These kids are emotionally decadent. They are so battered from the negative entities in their lives that they become numb to conscious thinking. They also need to understand patience. To be emotionally fit, they need patience. Patience will allow them to be confident in an unanticipated event, such as gang recruitership or peer pressure. It will help them to keep distracting thoughts from making them act foolishly. These are qualities that are needed in their lives if they are to grasp a real understanding of themselves and each other. They must fortify each other. They must learn to protect one another. If they are given the responsibility to protect their friends, to realize that by helping their friends stay safe, they aid themselves, then that camaraderie that is innate will provoke them to steer away from the nonsense. That costly lifestyle will not be able to penetrate their bond. They will influence each other in the safety of their bond that will ensure their friendship, which to them is life. What this is doing is reversing the snare of the gang ties. Instead of protecting their friends for a corrupt purpose, they will support them in a correct one.

A new standard must be set. Not by some political campaign or social analyst, but by the same people who desire to see these children do better. If nothing is expected of them, why would they be confident in anything? They must be assured of who they are by

111

the entire community. We must become more innovative in how these teens view the real world.

The youth have a lot of great questions. But they need reassuring answers to spiral them into productivity. They need it by the immediate people in their lives as well as the distant. I know a lot of young men that believe that you can only do certain things if you are a specific hue. They think that you have to be Latin to speak Spanish, white to understand stocks, and black to be a real gangster. Yes, stereotypical crap.

Inspiration needs assurance. When these minds become inspired, they need help. If no one is there to nudge them, to open their minds, or to give them the required resources, then why would they believe that they could be an engineer or business owner? They don't know any! Americans cannot continue to just move forward and think that youth crime is a fad or does not affect them. Our youth are being destroyed as the rest of the world pushes forward. Although our history, all of our history, has its dark and shameful points, this country was built upon the confidence of people to persevere and believe in the greatness of God, themselves, and their country. This president (Obama) loves education. Inspiration pours out of him. He believes in the children and desires to invest in them as our greatest asset. Do you believe that he is wrong? So why would you not invest in our children? All of our children.

We are the ones making the decisions. Average working parents with average children will decide the future of our world. Not the esoteric belief of the elite. Don't allow your children to believe that they have no place in this world. We are all interdependent and need someone else's help.

Growing into the real identity of manhood will allow them to recognize the errors of their life. Studying about real people, achieving real goals, will give them strength in their individuality. That "fish" trend of go with the group must be broken because if we are a nation that screams freedom, then those bonds of hopelessness must be destroyed by choice. These kids require inspiration from real men and women that will not breach their trust. Those people that can do a sincere job without forcing it are most reliable. Their confidence will increase in life as ours does.

The Idea Of Peace: What Is It?

Many of us desire peace in our neighborhoods, our country, our world, but do we really understand what we are requesting? Peace is not simply the absence of anarchy or chaos. There are more variables within this perspective. Before we can begin implementing peace within our neighborhoods, we must understand exactly what it is that we are invoking.

First, peace and happiness are equivalent. They are co-existent. In religion, your happiness is equaled to your relationship with the Creator. Peace is no different. Peace though, requires you to reveal the totality of who you are. These teens cannot perceive peace outwardly because they cannot feel it inwardly.

Do you know what it feels like to hate? Of course. The rage, the anger, although consuming and draining, is very easy to indulge. It is easy in our logic to lash out at the things that we cannot understand or control. They must learn that although they do not control the circumstances in which they were born, they can control the outcome of who they will become. They must witness this in others, which is why real idols must come from real neighborhoods. Their plight cannot be justified by their behavior. Their behavior must not be encouraged because of their plight. Their feelings cannot be released through wild anger and rage. Some of these kids feel as though they are dying every day, only to be reborn in the night, to relive it.

You must teach them real happiness. How? Their health, beliefs, leisure time, and social interactions must be coherent. They need to see the balance. Showing them how one affects the other will help them understand the importance of patience, courage, and being alert.

I have asked many people this same question and surprisingly, I get a similar answer most of the time. I ask "What do you want out of life?" Most people usually reply, "To be happy". When I inquire more about defining this, a lot of people cannot. They want to be happy, but they do not know how. We all want to be happy but there is no set standard for what makes a person happy. If you are a happy person, then you have found that which makes you happy. You have your peace. Another person may simply not know and what makes you peaceful, may not work for them. What you can do is help them to search for what it is that they need. Help them to understand what they need in their life to encourage them.

Children that grow up in dangerous neighborhoods have no understanding of real peace because they are surrounded by chaos. They believe that this is life. In some poor neighborhoods, roaches are a common encounter. When you would visit someone's home that did not have them, you thought that something was wrong with them. Roaches in the home seemed normal. The same happens when you are immersed in crime and violence. It is acceptable because it is frequent.

They need things that will invoke happiness within them. They can be taught. There are things that some teens enjoy doing that are considered "goofy" or "nerdish", and for fear of isolation and ridicule, their good habits never receive confident support. They cannot just be taken outside of the neighborhood, shown something, then plunged right back into the chaos. For some, this may work, for most, where there is no support; they fall into what they are familiar with.

They really have no concept of what they are looking for only to satisfy some temporary gratification. I know that sometimes it is difficult for adults to define happiness when surrounded by poverty and dissension, but it cannot be limited to material wealth. We can't allow our happiness and standards to be set by candied elements. Although they do not define us, they can overwhelm us.

You cannot simply take these young adults out of their rebellious lifestyles and expect for them to change because you have threatened them. A structure must be set. A standard established for their interests. Not one set by the bureaucrats that don't have any interaction with them, but one designed by the people that truly have a solid interest within these communities. Strip these areas of their decadence, not just physically, but ideologically, and you can transform the minds of the people. Right now, churches are the last strongholds within these areas, but the youth, see these places as old people institutions. The youth are very active and institutions must be built (or reorganized) that will evolve with their attention. Not just a recreational center, but an institution that guides that energy, takes out the irrationality of their anger, and prove to them that they are worthy of great achievements. They need more than just hope. They need to know what happiness is to them and that they can enjoy their lives in a productive way. They need real experience in agendas that matter. If we want them to be prideful and accepting of who they are, then they need to accomplish things that matter to them and their community. Encourage their innovation and creativity. It is there, hidden under the mask of social acceptance.

You do not want your children to grow up with the hardships that you had? You do not want them to fall into a bad lifestyle? Then truly invest in their future. Our world is so advanced, so connected that we must spread the truth about happiness. We may live in the wealthiest country but we are so unappreciative of life. Our diets, our communication with one another and our negligence of each other attest to this.

Kids in underdeveloped neighborhoods see the glamour of capitalism and figure that they have to take it to get it. They have no hope already, thus they have nothing to care for and nothing to lose. Even though racism may not be a prevalent factor in their lives, they still feel as though they are unequal. You see it with white children's anger towards the system. Deficient in material things makes them feel cheated. Feelings from past tensions begin to arise in them. They are unsettled because in America, if you do not have the latest accessories, you are ridiculed and laughed at. No one wants to be made fun of. No one wants to be a nobody. So, to retain that sense of happiness, you do what you understand to obtain those things that make you feel equal.

Freedom in a Democracy does not mean without rules. We do not want to trample on our freedoms as a Democracy, but we cannot allow anarchy to hide under the guise of freedom. The youth need to understand that their liberties were given to them by God and because of the sacrifices and decisions of their ancestors, no matter the hue of the family. It is something that must be appreciated and not abused. Abusing your freedom will only inhibit your happiness.

In the streets, money is referred to as dust. I don't know why, but considering how it comes and goes, I think that it is appropriate. We put so much work into becoming rich, that once any sense of wealth is obtained, we still find that we are miserable. You have so many variables to worry about that you do not even get to enjoy your possessions. You become a slave to money. The money will decide how you will live. When you will sleep, eat, and how vicious you will become to protect it. Thinking back, it really is an addiction. Some people will stay outside, selling drugs all day, until they reach a specific amount. Others will travel to various areas to procure the profit. It becomes so habitual that if you do not comply, you feel unfulfilled.

Insanely, we thought that making money would free us from rules and depression. We were not stupid. We knew that the actions that we decided were our choice. We just did not realize that the seriousness of our actions would strip us of our happiness. That is what I am clarifying. Happiness has been lost in the expression of wealth. Feeling good about yourself seems to be only true for those that have the materials to manifest it. Happiness has been given a specific criteria; a certain appeal that is defined outside of ourselves. If you have certain properties and materials, then you can be happy. Absent from these objects means that you are isolated from the happiness that the rest of the world enjoys. Depression breeds war. These kids are no different. They simply grow up into angry adults.

Being young, we are always anxious. This can cause a teen to be in a continuous race. I know that this is the natural state for the youth to be full of energy and rushing everything, but this can cause them to become depressed, discouraged, and beaten. Youthful energy is an addiction as well. You get so intoxicated from it that everything almost seems surreal.

A great many teens today do not understand what the benefits are of being patient. The tolerance, strength, and courage that are involved are void to them. It is also not just an old and young factor because there are older people that are inept when it comes to patience. But, they must learn it from a beneficial perspective in order to respect it. This is a learned attribute that is critical for life. These kids want everything in the now and care nothing about the later.

Having peace means growing up in an environment that does not tell you that because your father was a drug dealer, that you will be one as well. That just because your past is shaky, does not limit who you are and can be. They must realize that their lives are more than just entertainment. These depressed areas require real innovation by real people. These kids believe that if you are not born with privilege that you will not matter. It is not all their fault. Adults have an outdated system that has overlapped onto itself. The snares of the past continue to rob the future. They kids need to have some concept of time within life.

What is happiness? What does it mean for these kids? What is it for the adults living in these areas? It is reiterated over and over. There must be people within these environments to electrify that happiness. Happiness is defined differently by everyone. We must build those environs that will incubate this into reality.

The isolation must be broken—that separation that divides them from the rest of the world. They are bound by their sense of belonging. They cannot obtain happiness ostracized from everyone else. That yoke that they carry is unnecessary. How can they possibly have happiness if they continue to carry the burdens of their parents? The parents are supposed to help the children carry their burdens, not the opposite.

If all that they view is the misery of the world, why the heck would they want to live in it? Adults are so busy trying to make the perfect life that the ones that should benefit from it, do not. These kids are miserable because we are miserable. They follow our disastrous mistakes that we attempt to shield them from. Information is so widespread that you cannot protect them from all of the bad ideas in the world but you can prepare them for what may come. Do not act as though good and evil do not exist. This only allows wicked things to be more exotic and alluring. Allow them to understand why they exist and why they should choose the path of good.

Suffering touches everyone and showing these kids that being appreciative of themselves and others will allow them to experience it realistically.

The design of real peace within our neighborhoods and the lives of the youth is not some vague concept beyond our grasp. It must be understood and applied. These kids have no idea just how much control that they truly have over their own happiness.

Once the idea is understood, the invoking process can begin. We must teach these kids that they are the perpetrators of their own misery and they must become the innovators of their own happiness. To produce a desired result means that we, as adults, must be effective in the lives of our children if we want their lives to be happy. Show them how to enjoy their life because you enjoy them in your life. Reciprocating your inward happiness outward will allow you to be more receptive to the living.

The Idea of Peace......Not just an Idea.

The Idea of Peace: The Recovery

What do we need to do that will effectively bring about peace in our neighborhoods? We must take the "hood" out of neighborhood and reinforce neighbor. Darkness (ignorance) only last as long as allowed to. You must not allow these people to continue controlling your home, your lives, or your children anymore. These bogus ideas and dreams must be revealed by you. Know your neighbors. Know who lives in your area. I understand that everyone wants privacy but too many secrets allows for danger to fester. You love your child? Then make it your duty to work with others to improve the conditions of your area. And just because an area looks nice does not mean that it does not have a gang problem. Anyone familiar with Chicago knows that Hyde Park is a really upscale area but it is gang oriented as well. Stop allowing people to tell you that the gang problem cannot be stopped. Just as they began, they will see their end.

If you sit out of the game, then you are just as guilty. Anyone that believes in the Bible, the Qur'an, or life is bound to truth. Your children should fear and respect you, not the dealer on the corner. Why? Because the dealer on the corner should fear you. He should fear getting too close to your home. He should be hiding from you and eventually when he sees that there is no where safe on any part of the block to hang out, he will disappear. You must enforce this. You must be persistent and diligent. Take turns with your neighbors. Sit out front of your homes and ask the police to patrol more. Do not allow the gangs to barricade you in your home. You and your children are not the prisoners.

State officials and law enforcement work for you. They are your investment. Use that investment to protect your "nest egg", which are your children. Make the media shame all criminal acts. Destroy the perception of the hood as glamorous chaos. To give your children the joy of growing up, you must get your hands bloody (not literally). Peace comes with work. Once you have shown your children how to be happy within themselves, they can teach it to their peers. They will apply what they know. They affect each other more than you know. Although our circumstances make us believe that we are in control of nothing, we have to understand that all things began with an idea, just as they all dissipate back into that origin. All of the gangs, the street life, the crime, all came from a thought. They all began within someone and it will take that same spark to destroy these flawed ideas. Not everyone involved in the street life enjoys what they are doing. Some are just good at it and others are just looking to survive. Our culture teaches us that living means that you must have the prettiest car, clothes, home, and accessories. Our description of life is "materials are what matter". This is what they understand. These tangible items are what these teens recognize. As it is consistently reiterated to them, they see it as the truth to their existence. Life seems to only be exciting when they have stuff. They shouldn't believe that because they do not have certain items that their life is unworthy. The true value of their lives must be recovered from the false idea of acceptance.

Peace is a reflection of balance. Peace is perfection. I know that many of us don't believe in perfection but it simply attest to a system performing in completion. We must form peace within and then display it daily. It has to be reared and molded within these communities. Simply marching and rallying won't suffice. These were effective tools at the time they were implemented but these gangs are not affected by this. There must be another tactic employed to fight this disease. Communities must network together. There must be a strong link, neighbor to neighbor, for it to work. Everyone (or most) must be involved and the goal must be the same; to save that which was lost—our children's freedom to grow up. Neighborhood watch signs are ineffective because after a while, you realize that no one is really watching. Sit on your porches. Show them who you are and what you are not willing to tolerate. Not just some of the time, none of the time. If your neighbor is elderly and has an out of control teen, you need to step in because like I said before, they will infect your child. Trust me, it spreads very easily.

The weak positions in these areas must be secured by the people that live in them. People need to start walking around the adjacent areas, getting to know one another, setting up an itinerary where people from every block within a specific area meet and implement designs that benefit the community. I surely do not suggest that you place yourself in the way of harm or danger, but if your neighborhood is drug infested, then you are in the way already. I stress unification with the neighbors because this cannot be won by one person or a few. Just as the bangers protect each other, so must you and your neighbors. The book of Proverbs (3:29) teaches that your neighbor is with you for safety. It is your duty to protect your neighbor and they in turn protect you.

This is the application of peace; A community functioning in solidarity for a desired result. The gangs are simply a proxy for another person's control of their wealth. Do you really want to live in fear while someone else benefits from it? Should these people live wildly and wealthily while you suffer in the shadows? You haven't done anything wrong and you should not be oppressed or fear for your children. Your neighbors need to trust in you and you in them. Correct that bond and do not allow fear to intrude on it. Peace is within you and it must be formulated outside of you and spread. But in spreading it, do not allow your own peace to be offset by the outside influences.

If there are no hard times in these "hoods", how can violence be praised in the entertainment world? It wouldn't be real to speak about it if the violence wasn't paramount. We must completely change the ideology of these areas. I am not talking about some revolution, but evolution. Too many years have hardships, sorrow, hopelessness, and hunger, been pivotal points for the criminal element to find sanctuary. Too much protection is given to bad elements and ideas within these communities. We must move forward and shed ourselves from the slavery of violence and corruption, and to do so will take unifying, not solely of religion or hue, but for the common purpose of life. The assurance of our children, of our lineage, must be secured. Life must be breathed back into these decadent areas. Positive ideas can have more influence than negative ones. When negative reinforcement is destroyed, doing the productive thing is not so difficult.

Some people are simply talking or wishing to help these children. It takes for us to put aside our fear and go into these areas and take control. One person or element will not work. Just as there are many variables in the streets, there must be multiple variables to combat it. Have you noticed that the dealers know that the police cameras are there yet they continue to sell drugs (even in the daylight)? Nothing replaces the human element of survival. When the desire for survival is initiated, people can do some really stupid things. You get lost in the world. You see it all the time with men that leave prison, swear not to come back, and soon return. They forget about this place, and when I say forget, I mean that they put it out of their scope and are negligent to its reality. Prison is introspection. It forces you to analyze everything. That is why so many people can truly believe in change when they are incarcerated. They may honestly be sincere at that moment but when they return back into the mess that they previously left, it becomes easy for them to become acclimated into that life again, which is why these areas must be reclaimed. Incarceration only puts you in abeyance. Many of these men believe that the outside world is the same as when they were initially locked up. But the problem is double sided because even when there are programs, people still recidivise and society is tired of being hurt when a hand is extended. See, it is not simply a governmental or law-enforcement problem, but a cultural one. But outside influences cannot necessarily stop it. It is a requirement of an inward implosion to curb it. The inner core is just not strong enough because of the divisions amongst the people.

People that are directly affected must be the core. They must be the pivot that allows for change to happen but they mustn't allow the sanctity of their connection to be uprooted.

As I presented earlier, not a revolutionary, but an evolutionary process is what we require. Infiltrate these communities with local investors and investments. If these communities are restructured by the people living in these areas, then there will be more confidence in the decisions being made. We have become inept in our duties within these neighborhoods and have allowed them to fail in our absence.

I believe that if there are more visible outlets to improve life, to prove to them that applying your ideas in real life can be beneficial and self-fulfilling, then they will become more involved. Of course there will be those dissidents that will be against improvement because they make their living off of the corruption but they cannot be a deterrent. But if the majority works together, relentlessly, then there will be no room for these anarchists to keep up their acts.

Our sons and daughters are dying drastically and it will take drastic changes to save them. This struggle does not need to be one of bloodshed but of persistent activity. Don't misunderstand me, I believe in God, but these teens are not receptive to that (at least not in the effective sense). They avoid God because faith is too complicated for them. You pray to God and ask him to grant you effective tools to teach and save these kids. You ask for the strength and entities in which to apply truth. Money cannot be the only answer. They must learn that money itself is not the key but the proper application of it partially brings about happiness. Help them recover the confidence of who they need to be. They just don't know.

I do not know how many are actively involved but I believe that any rapper that is making money, talking about the hood, should be actively involved in changing the hood. And those that are doing something should be acknowledged for it. The only time that we see these rappers splattered across the news is when they fall out of grace into some nonsense. Exploit the good that some of them do. If they do charity, promote it. Let the youth see that these guys are not all greedy. Allow them to use their celebrity to intervene in the lives of these kids. That is part of their job description even if they don't want it to be. Hence, that is what needs to be done. Call these guys out and make them get involved. Everyone, not just entertainers, must be accountable. Those that are in prison and those coming out of prison, should be held responsible for the nonsense that was displayed. Stop supporting people that are diligent in doing bad things. I know that it is difficult with loved ones when you do not want to abandon them, but when it matters to your child's life, support the decision that will help your child. And I am not saying that people in prison do not need help to change but if they are not actively changing that conditioned stance in themselves, then they will continue to be harmful to you and themselves. Do not support this. Aiding someone in their depravity is not loving them. Do not support nor tolerate corrupt ideas or actions. This goes against the natural survival instincts within you.

Now, let us take a look at supply and demand within the drug scheme. I cannot answer for the demand position, as I am not an ex-addict, but from the supply side, I can attest that it can be quelled from a dealer's perspective. Those dealers that are in it for monetary gain can be dissuaded with more lucrative avenues if they are tangible to them. Drug dealers are businessmen (albeit illegal) but they are that. They want to live better than they are accustomed to. It is just so easy to go out and sell drugs (they think) which makes it so appealing. But as I pointed out earlier, they do not consider the market risk. Show it to them from a monetary perspective: e.g.

First- Let's say that the average street dealer makes $1,500 a week (which many do not). Now, in a month they will make $6,000, (counting margin of error for losses). Now, shorts are considered a normal loss, for example, $8 for a $10 bag or two $10 bags for $15. In a year's time at this pace, they could make $72,000 (if they never move up in weight). Sounds great! But, let us take in the cost of living on this side. They need food, clothes, guns (for protection of course), car, re-cop money, bond money, and lawyer money. Plus seeing how they are so sexually involved, they tend to have children. That $72,000 doesn't seem so extravagant now, especially if a person is caught and has to spend time in jail. See, jail is a big interruption into their 5-year plan. Trust me, nobody gets that rich from selling drugs that they cannot be touched. All of the big time figures have fallen. But that's the scam. You continue to fall into the cycle and you never really get on solid foundation.

You want to stop the kids from selling drugs? Then you really have to show them why it is more beneficial to have a 30-year plan than a 5-year scheme. Take them to places that will prove to them that they can succeed. But we must also invest in these areas that are a breeding ground for their hopelessness. There needs to be a physical restructuring as well as a mental. Use the businesses in your neighborhood to reinvest back into the community. If they do not, then don't give them your business. These community leaders must come together with, not only local businesses, but schools and churches to form a network that solely focuses on community improvement. Involve the children in this. They will appreciate their ideas more and will be inspired to open up. Show them exactly what it means to live. Stop leaving the entire burden up to law enforcement. Don't wait for the politicians to enact stronger policies simply to keep people locked away longer. That isn't stopping the problem. Look at the news. The prison population is still at an enormity. Every year, we have newer, harsher laws enacted to attempt to deter crime. It hasn't seemed to be that effective. Most of these kids know nothing of the law nor the severity of what they face by committing these crimes.

These communities must be salvaged by more than just hope. The youth have no endurance for hope. Spiritual leaders can only be effective if they can relate. That means that you require leaders that can talk to them realistically without trying to spook them into belief. Parents must be more knowledgeable about what is happening in their children's lives. People must be more informed with the affairs of their communities. There must be a balance set for these kids. If they are taught that God wants them to live poor and wretched lives, then they will shun any spiritual teachings. And they cannot be given a Biblical credit card, thinking that they have time to do what they want and all is forgiven. There must be a consequence to what they do.

Open activity within a community will quell the chaos. When more people are grouped together and involved with each other, bad influences tend to flee. They have no links to attach them to a positive flow, so they stand out with nowhere to hide.

That is why it is necessary for real business leaders to help with these communities. Most people in these areas only understand money in its physical sense. If they can be taught the real essence of money, investing, and business, then they will not be as slavish to it. They will better understand how to control it and not allow it to deprive them of their happiness.

There have been many community organizations, many different grants and programs designed to help the poor people, but what people on the outside cannot stop the anarchy and violence. It will take an entire seismic shift from the inside to change the direction of the generation. If all that they really know is what they have been taught, then they must see a total reformation from those that have done (and failed) what they are attempting to do in cohesion with those that are in positions to make progress tangible in these neighborhoods. No one holds the patent on good ideas and the youth must be involved with this process. The neighbors in these areas must be the innovators to stop the killings. They are the people that understand the amount of stress that these areas can take. They know what will and will not be seen as invading. Actions in these communities cannot appear incursive or there will be rebellion. This is why brute force will not work. Police in the past have believed that force would work but it only fed the idea of police as the enemy. This is why you will have gangs fighting back the police. Killing them becomes included as a necessary tactic, although it is wrong. And with excessive force, residents see brutality because someone innocent always gets hurt. Police are wound so tight that they have no real effective ability. They do not want to be the bad guys but they also don't want to appear weak to these gangs. They need support from all sides because it must be very stressful trying to save someone that does not seem to want your help. But they can only do so much as they are permitted to or it will cost them.

Remember, the youth only want what we all want. They just want to feel as though they matter in this world. They just don't realize that they are someone loved and worthy of it. We must show them that at every interval of life, there are benefits. Not just adulthood, but being a teenager has its highlights to. Likewise, we cannot allow them to detest growing up; being miserable around them all the time will give them the idea that adulthood is burdensome. You, the parent, the uncle, the teacher, the aunt, the leader, must direct their path. I understand that this may not be a well paying position with money but it is definitely fulfilling within the humanistic value. And this has its rewards as well. You must not let go of them. Do not surrender to them unless you are willing to accept the responsibility for their decisions. I didn't think that you would want to.

To a point, law enforcement must be given credit for breaking the backs of the gangs. They have effectively taken out the leadership and disoriented the followers but there was not sufficient enough structure in place to direct them into better avenues. Communities must work together with their officials that believe in saving these kids instead of just locking them up. These kids are looking for someone to believe in that can really show them what to do. Not some pompous jerk looking to make a career. They need leaders that can relate to them and the world outside of theirs. They need peers that can attest to the true value of success. That means that they need people that they trust to guide them. This has to be done by people that have an intimate interest in these areas. It cannot be impeded by hue or class, but invoked by the true value of human camaraderie. That is the recovery. That is why it is essential for us to reclaim what we have forsaken. Not just a dream but the reality of that dream.

About The Author

Nicholas Malaki Crayton is an ex-gang member that is currently working to rebuild the conditioned battlefield that is the mind of the youth today. He is currently serving time for his own reckless behavior but has vowed his life in service to humanity and redemption.

Since his incarceration, he has obtained a bachelor's in Biblical Studies, an Associate's degree in Liberal Studies, Doctor's certificate in Motivation. African Hebrew Israelite certificate of Achievement, and multiple certificates from Crimnon International, including Personal Integrity, Way to Happiness, Conditions of life, and Crimnons Completion certificate.

Mr. Crayton is also affluent in Spanish and Biblical Hebrew. He taught Religious Education in Galesburg for three years and is an advisor to many who call him friend/brother.

www.ingramcontent.com/pod-product-compliance
Lightning Source LLC
Chambersburg PA
CBHW071001040426
42443CB00007B/608